DANBURY PUBLIC LIBRARY
Danbury, Conn.

Design & text: Mike Dillon

Photographs: Jim Linna

Blueprints: Mark Wolf

Lettering: Bruce Hale

Chapelle Ltd.
Owner: Jo Packham

Design/layout Editor: Leslie Ridenour

Staff: Marie Barber, Ann Bear, Areta Bingham, Kass Burchett, Rebecca Christensen, Holly Fuller, Marilyn Goff, Holly Hollingsworth, Shawn Hsu, Susan Jorgensen, Pauline Locke, Barbara Milburn, Linda Orton, Karmen Quinney, Cindy Stoeckl

If you have any questions or comments, please contact:

Chapelle Ltd., Inc.
P.O. Box 9252
Ogden, UT 84409
Phone: (801) 621-2777
FAX: (801) 621-2788
e-mail: Chapelle1@aol.com

Library of Congress Cataloging-in-Publication Data

Dillon, Mike.
   The great birdhouse book : fun, fabulous designs you can build /
Mike Dillon : photography by Jim Linna.
      p. cm.
   "A Sterling/Chapelle book."
   Includes index.
   ISBN 0-8069-9334-0
   1. Birdhouses--Design and construction.   I. Title.
QL676.5.D545 1999
690'.8927--dc21   98-48790
                                                         CIP
   598,072

10 9 8 7 6 5 4 3 2 1

A Sterling/Chapelle Book

Published by Sterling Publishing Company, Inc.
387 Park Avenue South, New York, NY 10016
© 1999 by Chapelle Ltd.
Distributed in Canada by Sterling Publishing
⅝ Canadian Manda Group, One Atlantic Avenue, Suite 105
Toronto, Ontartio, Canada M6K 3E7
Distributed in Great Britain and Europe by Cassell PLC
Wellington House, 125 Strand, London WC2R 0BB, England
Distributed in Australia by Capricorn Link (Australia) Pty Ltd.
P.O. Box 6651, Baulkham Hills, Business Centre, NSW 2153, Australia
Printed in China
All Rights Reserved

Sterling ISBN 0-8069-9334-0

Due to the limited amount of space available, we must print our patterns at a reduced size in order to give our patrons the maximum number of projects possible in our publications. We believe the quality and quantity of our patterns will compensate for any inconvenience this may cause.

The written instructions, photographs, designs, patterns, and projects in this volume are intended for the personal use of the reader and may be reproduced for that purpose only. Any other use, especially commercial use, is forbidden under law without the written permission of the copyright holder.

Every effort has been made to ensure that all of the information in this book is accurate. However, due to differing conditions, tools, and individual skills, the publisher cannot be responsible for any injuries, losses, and/or any other damages which may result from the use of the information in this book.

Contents

For my friends, Brian & Linda Basset
—*They planted the seed for Flights of Fancy*

Weathered
Friends.

Design Theory

Building birdhouses can be a wonderful creative outlet for the individual who enjoys crafts or woodworking. Your creation can be functional as well as expressive. This book was conceived and produced, in part, as a builder's companion to a book that I created, which was published by Andrews McMeel, called *The Art of the Birdhouse—Flights of Fancy,* which is a photographic collection of functional whimsy. I try to use everyday observations as well as works by others as inspiration to guide me in my designs. You may see a painting style of one of the masters and be able to use their technique when decorating the surface of your birdhouse. Maybe you enjoy collecting and choose to use the objects that you collect to decorate the outside of your birdhouse.

Obviously, common sense must be used once you have decided where your creation will be displayed. I don't think that great-grandmother's heirloom handmade doilies would be appropriate on a birdhouse in the backyard next to the patio, but imagine how sweet the same birdhouse could look up on a shelf next to her photograph. The use of birdhouses as indoor decoration has become quite popular in recent years, and I believe that, instead of purchasing something that has been mass produced, you can create your own designs that reflect you.

Maybe you aren't the woodworking type—tools are unfamiliar to you. Well, there is no reason you can't purchase a simple structure and paint it or decorate it to make it your own. Ever wonder what to do with Aunt Marjorie's assorted buttons she has collected over the years? Maybe you have some old rusty tools in the garage. These can all be used for decorating a birdhouse. I have found that once you let loose enough to look at things in this manner, you will begin to see them in a different light.

This book was not written to teach basic or advanced woodworking methods and, although some information is given for customizing your birdhouse for a particular species, it also does not attempt to provide all the available information related to creating nesting boxes for birds. There are many books available that can guide you in these areas. What I do hope that this book will do is inspire you to explore your ideas and realize how easy it is to create your own functional work of art. Keep in mind if you are interested in attracting birds, what you may think is a pleasant decorative theme may only serve to scare the birds away. Some species have little or no taste. Study up on what will attract the bird you are looking for and modify your building or decorating accordingly.

Feel free to be creative and use the ideas and plans in this book as a visual resource. Birdhouses are a fantastic inspiration for using a variety of materials. Once you abandon traditional rules of birdhouse construction, the sky's the limit.

Mike Dillon

Darn Woodpeckers

6

Gallery of Ideas

There simply are not enough pages in this book to include instructions for building all of the birdhouses that I have designed. However, I wanted you to see the results of some more complex ideas that I came up with, such as constructing a set of urban brownstone apartment buildings for our fine feathered friends. Therefore, the photographs on pages 1–15 are provided as a gallery for additional inspiration as you create your own birdhouse.

How the Plans Work

For each of the projects outlined in this book, I provide a photograph of the completed birdhouse. Along with this, I also show you the parts in an "Exploded View" to illustrate how the parts fit together, and give you an idea of how to assemble the sides that you don't see in the photograph.

While I feel that the accompanying "Parts Diagram," including measurements, can be helpful, please do not feel that you must follow it exactly. If you are the type of person that has to follow directions to the letter, go ahead. But if you find a wonderful piece of aged barn wood that is an inch narrower than I've called for, by all means, use it. I promise that I won't come find you in order to question your design judgment. Remember, there are no rules!

In the instruction text, I will go into as much detail as I can without overwhelming you. If I mention a tool that you are not familiar with, you will see that I have tried to include a more common substitute, which may not work as easily, but will accomplish the task just as well. These instructions are more a description of the general process than they are step-by-step. Read the entire instruction page for each project before you start and you'll get the idea.

Materials & Methods

SAFETY—Always remember to wear the proper safety gear when working with tools. Goggles or safety glasses will protect your eyes. Earplugs are helpful when working with loud tools. The best rule for safety is take your time and use common sense. Don't use a tool that you are unfamiliar with. Learn how to use it properly.

WOOD—The type of wood that you choose can be instrumental in how your birdhouse is finished. I like to use recycled old wood whenever possible. Good sources for this may be an old dilapidated fence, a barn, or other old structures. Driftwood is an excellent material. However, it can often be hard to drill if it is dense. Rough-sawn cedar, which is commonly used in new fences, can be left to weather naturally or can be the cracked canvas for an interesting paint technique.

Plywood can work fine if it is exterior grade, which means it is made with a water-resistant glue. Notice that I say water resistant and not waterproof. No matter what materials you choose to work with, mother nature has a habit of proving that nothing is permanent. If you can't stand the thought of your creation changing over time, keep it indoors or under roof eaves. I personally enjoy what weathering will do over time. For example, an old, cut up, painted and weathered, wooden sign gives your structure a past life and provides a story to tell.

There are other types of wood that can work for interesting paint effects. Oriented Strand Board or OSB is a sheet material, like plywood, that is made out of large or small wood chips laminated together. On one side, the pattern can be quite pronounced and can be accentuated with paint. Medium Density Fiberboard, known as MDF, also comes in sheets. Not only does MDF have a smooth surface, but its cut edges don't have an obvious grain like plywood. This material does not work well outdoors, but it can be used on indoor projects where a smooth finish is desired. Bender board, which is made like plywood, is also sold in sheets and is made to form over curved surfaces. The thinner it is, the easier it is to bend.

CUTTING—There are a variety of tools available to use to cut out the parts—a table saw, band saw, miter or compound miter saw, jig saw, saber saw, ornamental scroll saw, radial arm saw, and various hand saws to name a few. I don't call for a specific type of saw in the project instructions unless there is a reason. If I named every saw possible for every cut, this book would be too heavy to carry.

If you are unfamiliar with any of these tools, please research their proper use or use a comparable tool that you are familiar with. Feel free to use whatever appropriate tool you have and are comfortable using. Again, safety is of utmost importance here. Don't attempt to use a tool that you are unfamiliar or uncomfortable with.

DRILLING—A hand-held electric drill will work just fine for any of the projects shown in this book. A drill press is helpful, although not neccesary. Drilling the entrance hole may be best accomplished with a paddle bit, hole saw, or a forstner bit. Many times I will wait until the structure is built before drilling this hole. It may be more obvious after you have completed the decorating that the hole looks better off center.

Depending on the type of bit you use, if you drill the hole after the birdhouse is assembled, you may end up with a small wood disk inside that rattles around. If you are desperate for entertainment, you can try to remove it. I usually just leave it inside, figuring that the birds won't mind.

Urban Flight

Flights of Fancy.

ASSEMBLY—Unless otherwise indicated in the individual project instructions, assemble the four sides first, overlapping the Back and Front over the two Side pieces. If you start with the Back first, it gives you a chance to get used to how the wood reacts to the fasteners you've chosen. Then attach the Front in the same manner.

Once the four sides are together, insert the bottom or attach the Base and Roof. Cut the bottom slightly smaller to help it go in easier. The cracks that are left where it meets the sides allow for drainage once you put it to use outside. For additional drainage, you may want to drill a couple of ¼" holes in the bottom. If you want the bottom removable for cleaning, use screws and no glue to attach it. Finally, attach the Roof and any remaining embellishments.

FASTENERS—When assembling your birdhouse, you may use nails, screws, or wood staples. Take care not to leave sharp tips of fasteners (that can cut you or the birds) exposed. Galvanized fasteners offer better resistance to the weather, as do brass or stainless steel screws. Use regular nails if you don't mind seeing the heads, finishing nails if you would rather have them less obvious. If you want to have easy access in order to clean out last year's nest, you may want to use screws to attach the roof, back, or base. Take care not to use fasteners too close to the edge of the wood to prevent splitting. It may be helpful to drill a small pilot hole first, slightly smaller than the fastener.

The pneumatic air stapler and brad nailer are wonderful time-saving inventions. However, these are operated by using an air compressor and, therefore, are not feasible for the average home hobbyist. If you are fortunate enough to have one or have access to one, you will find it to be quite useful.

ADHESIVES—Regular exterior-grade yellow wood glue will work for most projects. This may also be called aliphatic resin. Keep a damp rag handy to wipe up drips while they are wet. A hot-glue gun can come in handy and is designated in those projects where it is helpful. Be careful, it is called HOT glue for a reason. Cool-melt glue is a similar adhesive that becomes soft at a slightly lower temperature. Hot glue is usually not the best choice for exterior projects, but in the case of tile or stones, can be used to hold them in place until the mortar or grout is applied. It is an excellent adhesive if your project is to remain indoors.

WOOD PUTTY & SPACKLE—You may want to fill the nail, screw, or staple holes on your project, especially if you are going to paint it. On most of the birdhouses that I build for outside use, I don't worry about exposed fasteners. They just add to the charm of the birdhouse as they age. But for indoor creations, wood putty and spackle can be helpful. Spackle can be used on small nail holes, but in large cracks or holes, wood putty will do the trick. Always follow the manufacturer's instructions.

SANDING—A sheet of plain sandpaper can work wonders on a project. Wrapped around a square block of wood, it can sand flat surfaces. Tape or glue it around a dowel and it can be used to sand curves. There are many types of electric sanders available to make the job easier—belt, drum, disk, and orbital to name a few. The best approach when making a sanding choice is to decide what you need to accomplish and then find the appropriate tool.

PAINTING—Many great paint effects happen by accident. Don't be afraid to experiment. What's the worst that can happen? You can always repaint the parts that don't turn out as you had envisioned. In each set of instructions, I explain how the finish was achieved.

Latex house paint will work just fine for exterior use. If you question the durability of a particular paint or stain, try a test with polyurethane or varnish as a finish coat. Enamel or oil-based paint or stain isn't as pleasant to work with. But if you choose to use them, make certain to follow the manufacturer's instructions.

Spray paint, which is available in many colors in aerosol cans, can be used to achieve unlimited unique effects. It can be used to fade a color or spatter speckles.

For decorative finishes on indoor birdhouses, you will be able to use a variety of materials. Colored pencils or pastels may be used, but it is best to coat them with a clear finish. Test the finish first, as some materials may react to the type of finish you use. At your local hobby or lumber store, you will find a variety of aerosol spray or brush-applied clear protective fixatives or finishes.

MOUNTING—The method you use to mount your birdhouse may be as simple as a ¼" hole drilled in the back so it can hang on a nail in the wall. You may choose to hang it from a branch or overhang, using wire threaded through holes or eye screws.

Mounting the birdhouse to a post or pole can also work well. An easy way to mount it to the top of a post is to cut a square of plywood slightly smaller than the base of the birdhouse, and, using a couple of screws, screw it to the top of a wooden post. This makes a handy platform on which you can place the birdhouse. Use screws to attach it from below. Take care to use materials that won't rust or decay over time, unless, of course, the rusting is desired.

GETTING STARTED—You should now know enough to understand the instructions and be able to follow the Exploded View and Parts Diagram "blueprints" to design and fabricate your own "flights of fancy."

Red Sky at Night

For the Birds

Use the following table to customize your birdhouse and create a nesting box for the species you are trying to attract.

Species	Birdhouse Floor (inches)	Birdhouse Height (inches)	Entrance Height (inches)	Entrance Diameter (inches)	Height above Ground or Water (feet)	Preferred Habitat (codes[3])
Ash-throated Flycatcher	6 x 6	8–12	6–10	1½*	5–15	1, 5
Barn Swallow	6 x 6	6	([2])	([2])	8–12	6, 7
Bewick's Wren	4 x 4	6–8	4–6	1¼	5–10	2, 6
Bluebird	5 x 5	8–12	6–10	1½*	4–6	1
Carolina Wren	4 x 4	6–8	4–6	1½*	5–10	2, 6
Chickadee	4 x 4	8–10	6–8	1⅛	4–15	2
Downy Woodpecker	4 x 4	8–10	6–10	1¼	5–15	2
Golden-fronted Woodpecker	6 x 6	12	9	2	10–20	2
Great Crested Flycatcher	6 x 6	8–12	6–10	1¾*	5–15	1, 2
Hairy Woodpecker	6 x 6	12–15	9–12	1⅝	12–20	2
House Wren	4 x 4	6–8	4–6	1–1¼	4–10	2, 6
Nuthatch	4 x 4	8–10	6–8	([1])	5–15	2
Phoebe	6 x 6	6	([2])	([2])	8–12	6, 7
Prothonotary Warbler	5 x 5	6	4–5	1⅛	4–8, 3W	3, 4
Purple Martin	6 x 6	6	1–2	2¼	6–20	1
Red-headed Woodpecker	6 x 6	12–15	9–12	2	10–20	2
Robin	7 x 8	8	([2])	([2])	6–15	6
Titmouse	4 x 4	10–12	6–10	1¼	5–15	2
Tree Swallow	5 x 5	6–8	4–6	1½*	5–15	1
Violet-green Swallow	5 x 5	6–8	4–6	1½*	5–15	1

* Precise measurement is required; if the diameter is over 1½", starlings may take over the birdhouse.

[1] Brown-headed and pygmy nuthatches (1⅛"), red-breasted nuthatch (1¼"), and white-breasted nuthatch (1⅜") will all use the same birdhouse.

[2] One or more sides of the birdhouse should be left open.

[3] Preferred habitats. The numbers represent the habitat types listed:
1. Open areas in the sun (not shaded permanently by trees), pastures, fields, or golf courses.
2. Woodland clearings or the edge of woods.
3. Above water, or if on land, the entrance should face water.
4. Moist forest bottomlands, flooded river valleys, or swamps.
5. Semi-arid country, deserts, dry open woods, and wood edge.
6. Backyards and near buildings.
7. Near water, under bridges, or in barns.

Source: Homes for Birds pamphlet, Fish & Wildlife Service, U.S. Department of the Interior.

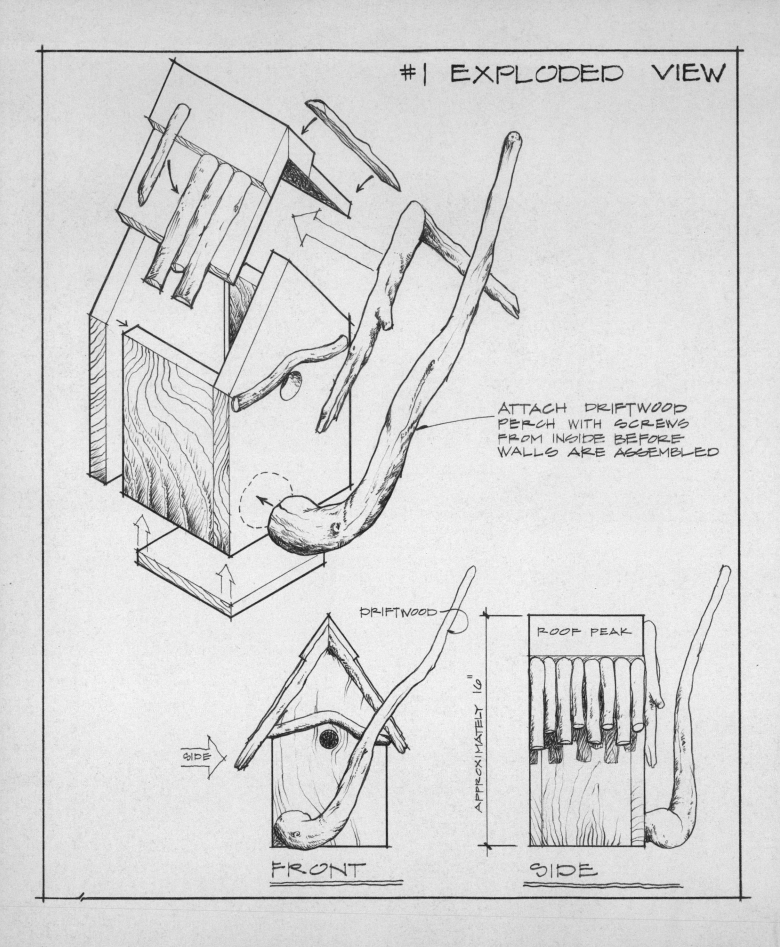

#1 EXPLODED VIEW

ATTACH DRIFTWOOD
PERCH WITH SCREWS
FROM INSIDE BEFORE
WALLS ARE ASSEMBLED

DRIFTWOOD

ROOF PEAK

SIDE

APPROXIMATELY 16"

FRONT

SIDE

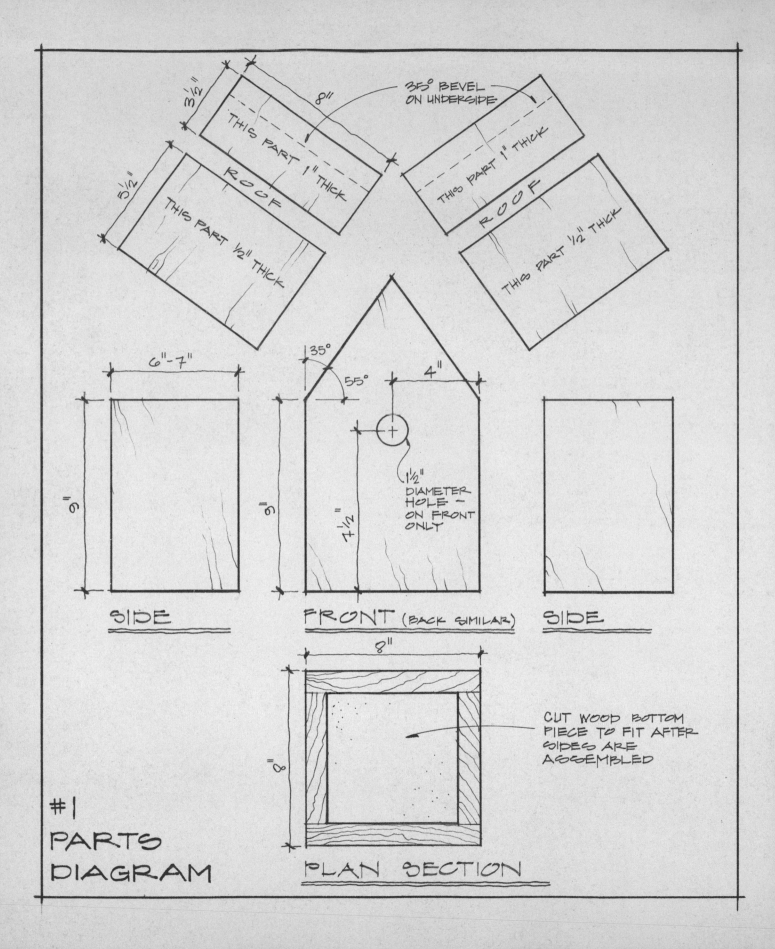

35° BEVEL
ON UNDERSIDE

3½"
8"
THIS PART 1" THICK
ROOF

5½"
THIS PART ½" THICK

THIS PART 1" THICK
ROOF
THIS PART ½" THICK

6"-7"
6"

SIDE

35°
55°
4"
6"
7½"
1½" DIAMETER HOLE — ON FRONT ONLY

FRONT (BACK SIMILAR)

SIDE

8"
8"

CUT WOOD BOTTOM PIECE TO FIT AFTER SIDES ARE ASSEMBLED

PLAN SECTION

#1
PARTS
DIAGRAM

TOOLS

Damp rag for glue drips
Drill
Drill bit for entrance
Hammer, screwdriver, or stapler
Saw

SUPPLIES

Assorted driftwood pieces
Nails, screws, or wood staples
Rough wood boards
Yellow wood glue

INSTRUCTIONS ————————————

• Saw the flat pieces from the wood boards. If possible, choose a board with a natural knot hole for the entrance. If not, drill the entrance hole on the Front now, or wait until the birdhouse is built and drill it last.

• I find it easier to assemble the four sides first, overlapping the Back and Front over the two Side pieces. If you start with the Back first, it gives you a chance to get used to how the wood reacts to the fasteners you've chosen. Apply glue to each joint as you assemble it. Keep a damp rag handy to wipe up glue drips while they are wet. If you want to hide the fasteners of the piece of driftwood used for the main perch, screw it on from the back side of the Front piece now. Then attach the Front in the same manner.

• If the sides don't go together square (which is common with old wood), take this opportunity to straighten the four corners by gently pushing or hammering it square while the glue is still wet. Once the four sides are together, insert the bottom. Saw the bottom slightly smaller to help it go in easier. The cracks that are left where it meets the sides allow for drainage once you put it to use outside. For additional drainage, you may want to drill a couple of ¼" holes in the bottom. If you want the bottom removable for cleaning, use screws and no glue to attach it.

• Next, attach the Roof pieces and the thicker, beveled Roof Peak pieces. Once these are on, you have a surface to which you can butt the ends of the driftwood pieces. Try to choose pieces that are no thicker than the Roof Peak pieces. These driftwood pieces can be rounded or carefully cut down the middle with a bandsaw so they have a flat side. You may find it easier to start nails in these driftwood pieces while they are on a flat surface and, once the fastener is almost through, put it in place to finish nailing. Attach driftwood pieces to the Front above the entrance hole and on the front and back of the Roof and Roof Peak pieces.

• The paint effect on this particular birdhouse was already on the old fence boards from which I built it. It was pure luck that the paint color was across the area of an existing knot hole. The driftwood could be substituted with sticks or branches with or without bark—just make certain to choose pieces that are not rotting.

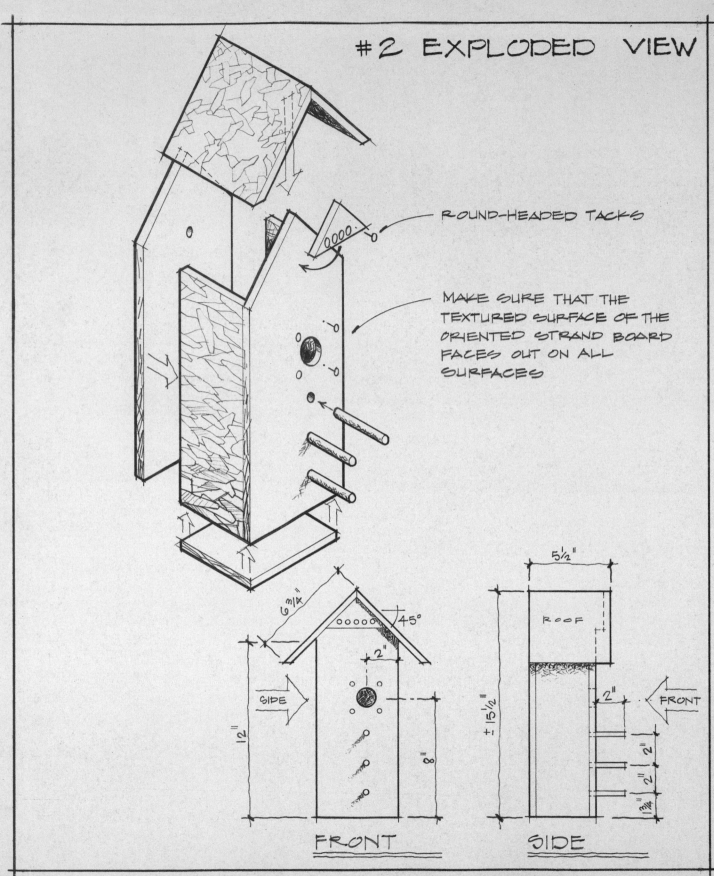

#2 EXPLODED VIEW

ROUND-HEADED TACKS

MAKE SURE THAT THE
TEXTURED SURFACE OF THE
ORIENTED STRAND BOARD
FACES OUT ON ALL
SURFACES

6 3/4"

45°

SIDE

12"

2"

8"

FRONT

5 1/2"

ROOF

± 15 1/2"

2"

2"

2"

3 1/4"

FRONT

SIDE

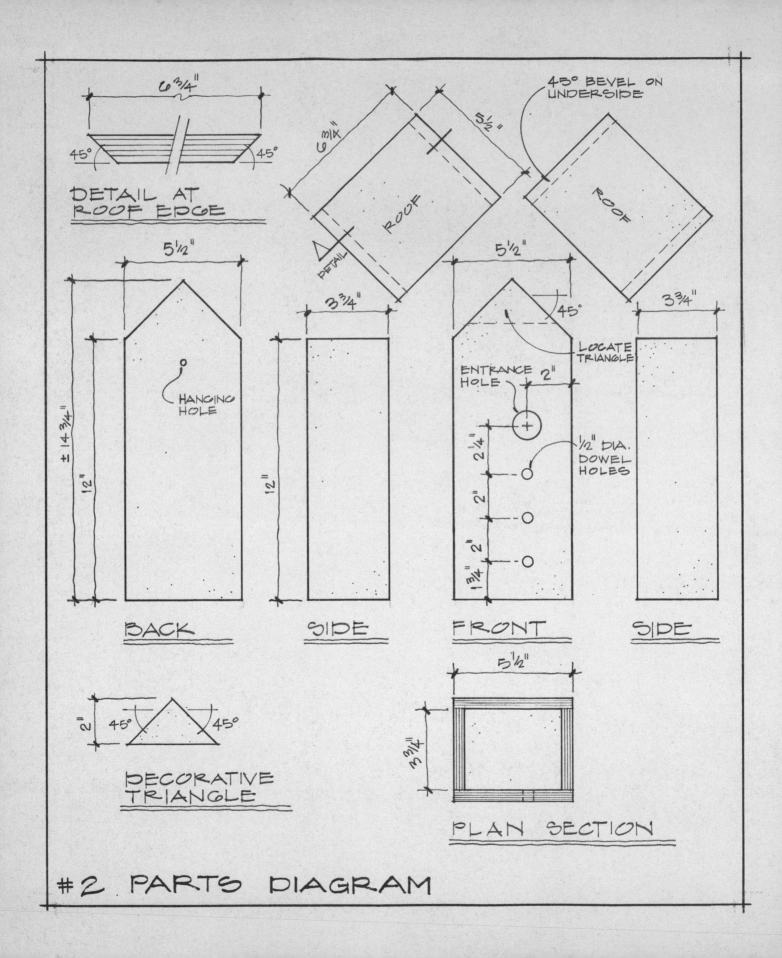

DETAIL AT ROOF EDGE

6¾"
45°   45°

45° BEVEL ON UNDERSIDE

6¾"   5½"
ROOF   ROOF

DETAIL

5½"
HANGING HOLE

BACK

3¾"
12"

SIDE

5½"
45°
LOCATE TRIANGLE

ENTRANCE HOLE   2"

½" DIA. DOWEL HOLES

2¼"
2"
2"
1¾"

FRONT

3¾"

SIDE

± 14¾"
12"

DECORATIVE TRIANGLE
2"   45°   45°

5½"
3¾"

PLAN SECTION

#2 PARTS DIAGRAM

2 TOOLS

Damp rag for glue drips
Drill
Drill bits for entrance and perches
Hammer, screwdriver, or stapler
Newspaper
Paintbrush
Sandpaper
Saw

SUPPLIES

Black latex paint
Copper, gold, and silver spray paints
Nails, screws, or wood staples
½" or ¾" OSB
Round-headed brass or silver tacks
½" wooden dowel (9")
Yellow wood glue

INSTRUCTIONS

• Saw the flat pieces from the OSB. Drill the holes on the Front for the three dowels and front entrance hole now, while the part can be held flat. Line up the Decorative Triangle with the roof line on the Front and attach it with glue and fasteners.

• When assembling the Front, Back, and Side pieces it is important to keep the rougher, more pronounced texture side out. Assemble the four sides with glue and fasteners. Insert the bottom piece and attach the Roof pieces, keeping the back of the roof flush with the back of the structure.

• Cut the dowel into three equal pieces. Don't worry if each dowel piece is slightly longer than you need. When the dowels are inserted, they can stick through the OSB on the inside of the birdhouse. Who knows, the birds may appreciate this as an inside ladder as well. It sometimes helps if you sand the end of the dowel around the edge to make it smaller, so it will fit into the hole easier. Spread a little glue on the side surface at the end of the dowel

you are inserting. Glue alone should be enough to hold the dowels in place without fasteners.

• Paint the whole birdhouse with black paint. Take care not to brush it on too thick as you don't want to fill in the texture. You may want to thin the latex a little with a tiny bit of water. Don't forget to paint under the eaves as well. Let the paint dry.

• Now comes the fun part. With the spray paints, one color at a time, spatter the whole birdhouse. This is best accomplished outdoors on a large area covered with newspaper. Holding a can of spray paint upright, lightly press down on the nozzle. Don't press hard—control is the key here. Experiment. If you hold it two or three feet away you should get some good-sized spatters. Light, short spurts work best. If you don't like the effect, paint the birdhouse black again and start over.

• After all the paint is dry, lightly hammer in the round-headed tacks where desired.

#3 EXPLODED VIEW

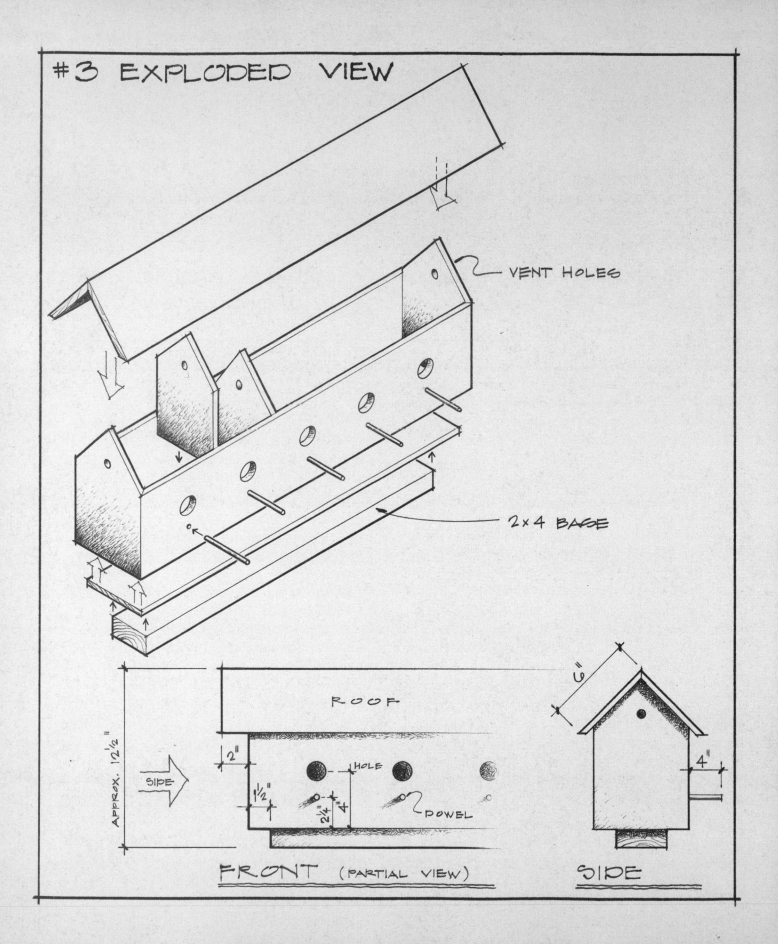

VENT HOLES

2×4 BASE

ROOF

2"

1½"

2¼"

4"

HOLE

DOWEL

APPROX. 12½"

SIDE

6"

4"

FRONT (PARTIAL VIEW)

SIDE

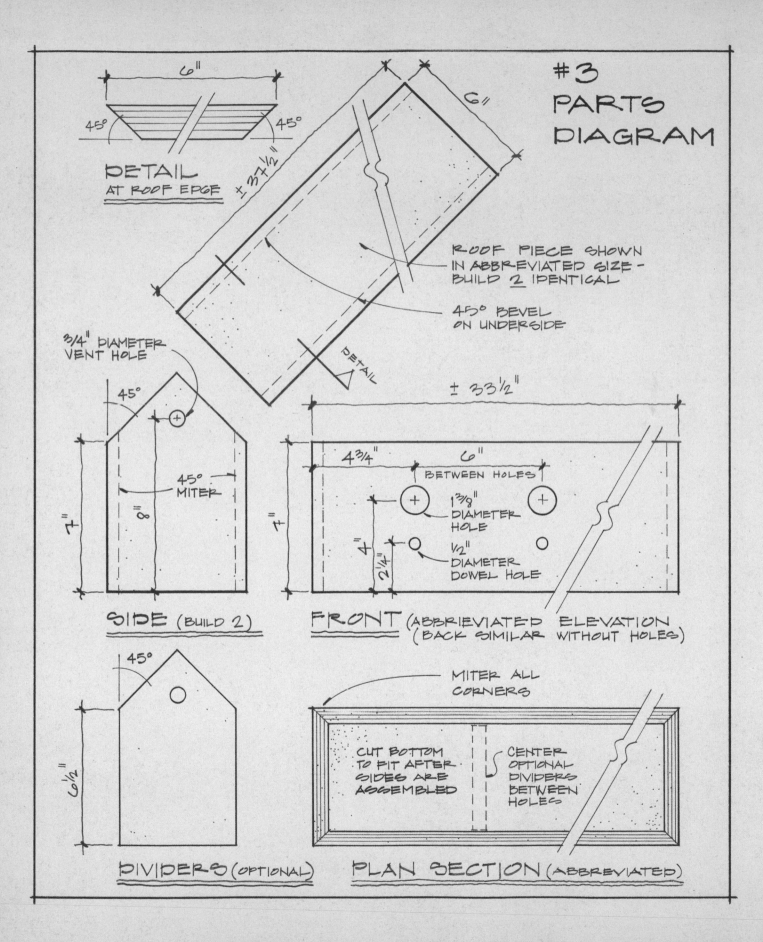

DETAIL
AT ROOF EDGE

6"

45°   45°

#3
PARTS
DIAGRAM

± 37½"

6"

ROOF PIECE SHOWN
IN ABBREVIATED SIZE -
BUILD 2 IDENTICAL

45° BEVEL
ON UNDERSIDE

DETAIL

3/4" DIAMETER
VENT HOLE

45°

45°
MITER

7"

8"

SIDE (BUILD 2)

± 33½"

4¾"

6"
BETWEEN HOLES

1³/₈"
DIAMETER
HOLE

7"

4"

2¼"

½"
DIAMETER
DOWEL HOLE

FRONT (ABBREVIATED ELEVATION
(BACK SIMILAR WITHOUT HOLES)

45°

9½"

DIVIDERS (OPTIONAL)

MITER ALL
CORNERS

CUT BOTTOM
TO FIT AFTER
SIDES ARE
ASSEMBLED

CENTER
OPTIONAL
DIVIDERS
BETWEEN
HOLES

PLAN SECTION (ABBREVIATED)

3 TOOLS

Damp rag for glue drips
Drill
Drill bits for entrance and perches
Hammer, screwdriver, or stapler
Paintbrush
Sandpaper
Saw

SUPPLIES

2X4
Latex paint
MDF, OSB, or Plywood
Nails, screws, or wood staples
Spackle or wood putty
½" wooden dowel (20")
Yellow wood glue

INSTRUCTIONS

• Saw the flat pieces from the sheet material. If you are building this house to be used by birds, cut out Dividers to separate each compartment. If it's only for decoration, you can skip this step. The beauty of this house is you can make as many (or as few) compartments as you like. I think that an odd number looks more balanced.

• Saw the 2X4 to length to be used as a base. Mark the Front and drill holes for the entrances and perches. I also drilled a medium sized hole towards the top of each Side and the top of each Divider for ventilation.

• Assemble the Front, Back, and Side pieces with glue and fasteners. Next, attach the bottom side of the bottom piece to the 2X4 base with glue and screws or nails. Insert the bottom piece, after applying glue to all the edges, into the birdhouse and then use fasteners to secure it in place. Once it is assembled this far, insert the Dividers. If they are cut to fit snug, you can just glue them in place. Since I was going to paint this one I wanted as few nail holes as possible.

• Attach the Roof pieces to the birdhouse with glue and fasteners. If you want to hang this one on a wall, cut the back Roof piece narrower so it can fit flush to the wall.

• Cut the dowel evenly into as many pieces as you have compartments. Don't worry if each dowel piece is slightly longer than you need. When the dowels are inserted they can stick through the front on the inside of the birdhouse. Who knows, the birds may even appreciate this as a ladder. It sometimes helps if you sand the end of the dowel around the edge to make it smaller, so it will fit into the hole easier. Spread a little glue on the side surface at the end of the dowel you are inserting. Glue alone should be enough to hold these in place without fasteners.

• Fill all the nail holes with spackle or wood putty. Once dry, sand lightly. Paint the outside as desired. I painted this one with a paintbrush, blending the colors while they were wet—not too wet though, or you'll be fighting drips.

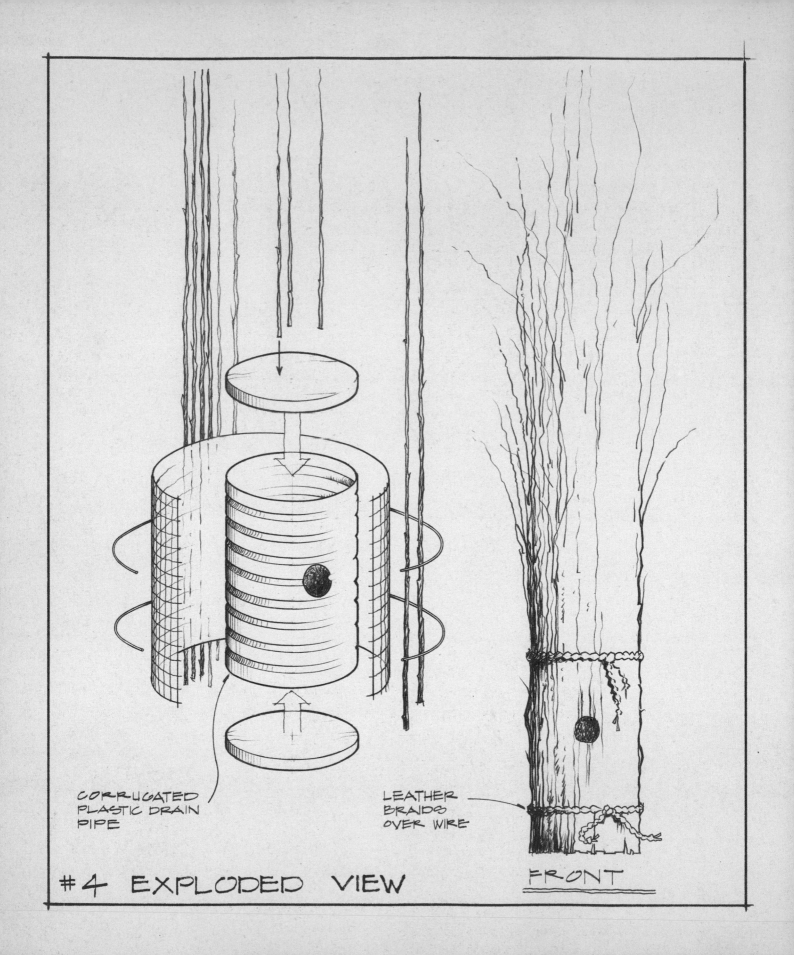

CORRUGATED
PLASTIC DRAIN
PIPE

LEATHER
BRAIDS
OVER WIRE

#4 EXPLODED VIEW

FRONT

House of Twigs

#4 PARTS DIAGRAM

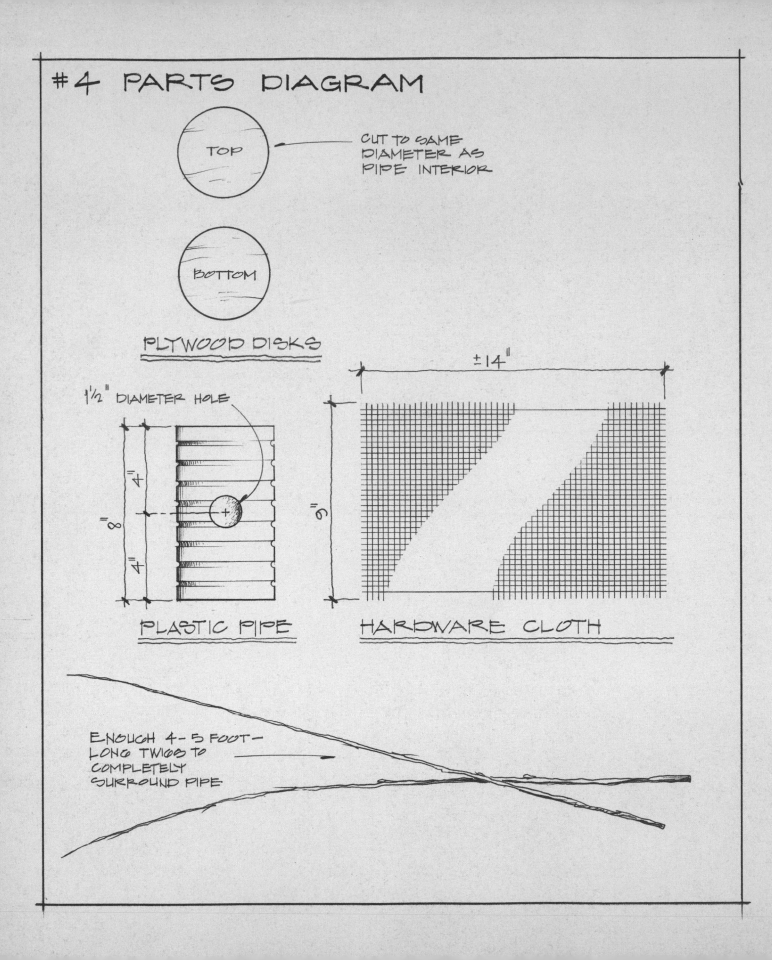

TOP

CUT TO SAME DIAMETER AS PIPE INTERIOR

BOTTOM

PLYWOOD DISKS

1½" DIAMETER HOLE

4"

8"

4"

PLASTIC PIPE

±14"

6"

HARDWARE CLOTH

ENOUGH 4-5 FOOT-LONG TWIGS TO COMPLETELY SURROUND PIPE

4 TOOLS

Drill
Drill bit for entrance hole
Hammer or stapler
Hot-glue gun and glue sticks
Metal snips
Pliers
Saw
Work gloves

SUPPLIES

Leather braids
Metal hardware cloth mesh
Nails or wood staples
Plastic drain pipe
Plywood
Twigs
Wire

INSTRUCTIONS ———————————

• This birdhouse requires a little bit of patience, but I think it's worth it. Start by cutting the Plastic Pipe to length. I used black plastic corrugated drain pipe available at home improvement or hardware stores. Saw Plywood Disks to fit in each end of the pipe and nail in place. Glue isn't necessary as it wouldn't stick well to the plastic anyway. Drill the entrance hole into one side of the pipe. It will help if you first drill a small hole at the center of where you want the entrance to keep the big drill bit from slipping. Go easy because it is tricky drilling into a corrugated surface that is curved as well.

• Working with metal hardware cloth mesh is best done while wearing work gloves. It can be nasty stuff. Wrap the hardware cloth around the pipe as snug as possible. Leave about an inch overhanging the top and bottom beyond the length of the pipe. Staple or nail through the plastic into the plywood and bend the nails over the hardware cloth before you nail them all the way in. Using the metal snips, cut the hardware cloth about every inch or so and bend it over to the plywood surface. Staple these flaps down to the plywood. Cut the hardware cloth at the entrance hole. Bend loose wires back with pliers so there aren't sharp wires that can cut you or the birds.

• Now, take the twigs and hot-glue them around the outside. They don't have to be even at the bottom—it's pretty easy to cut them even once you are done. You don't have to glue each and every one—they can be clumped. Cover right over the entrance hole. Cut shorter twigs and glue the ends of them to the top wood disk.

• Wrap around the birdhouse with wire in two or more places to hold all the twigs. Don't twist the wire too tight or you'll cut the twigs with it. Tie the leather braids over the wire. Use hot glue, if needed, to help hold the braids in place.

• Cut the bottom even, but slightly longer than the structure, and cut out the entrance hole, using the metal snips, garden snips, or a small serrated knife. You may need to glue extra pieces of twig around the entrance hole to clean it up.

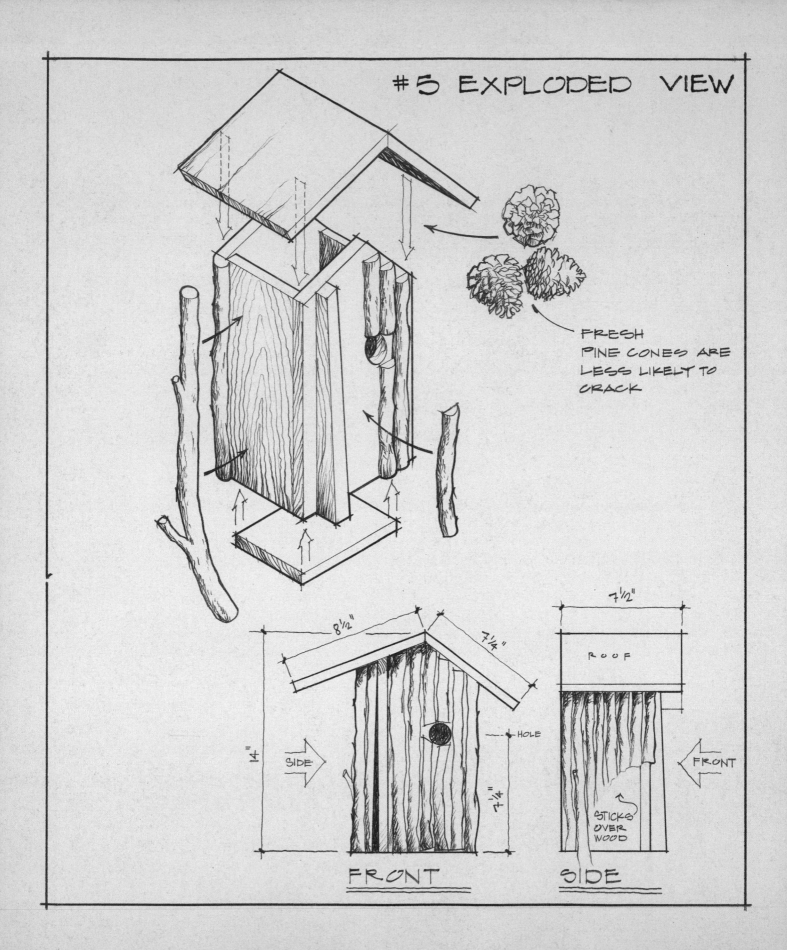

#5 EXPLODED VIEW

FRESH PINE CONES ARE LESS LIKELY TO CRACK

8½"

7¼"

14"

SIDE →

7¼"

← HOLE

FRONT

7½"

ROOF

← FRONT

STICKS OVER WOOD

SIDE

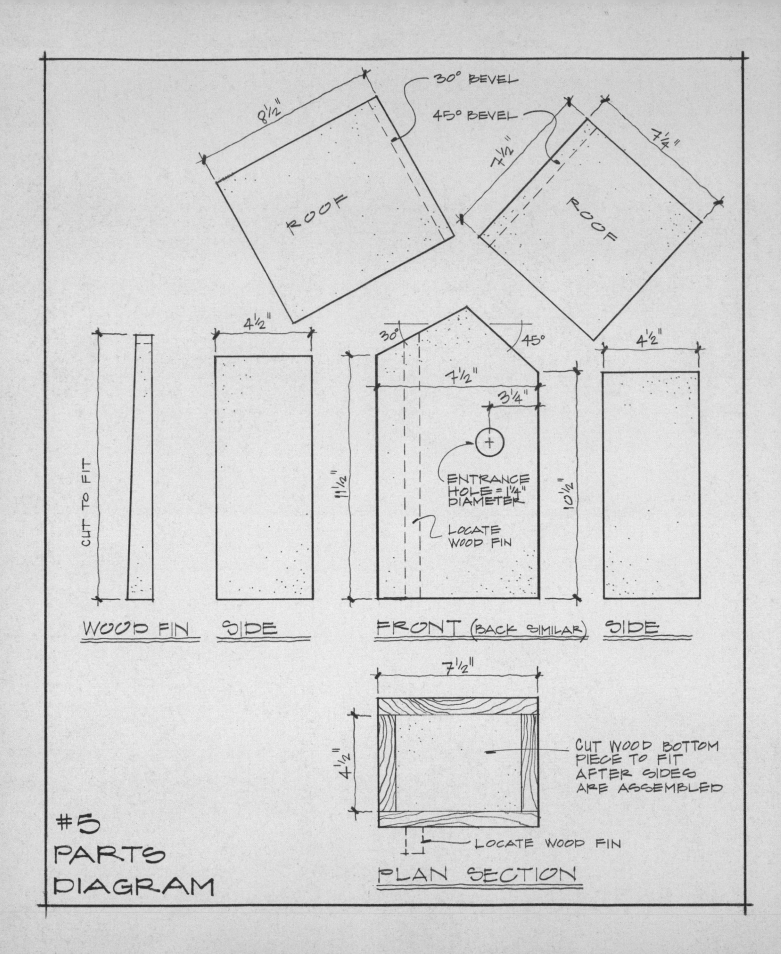

8½" 30° BEVEL

ROOF

45° BEVEL

7½" 7¼"

ROOF

CUT TO FIT

WOOD FIN

4½"

SIDE

30° 7½" 45°

3¼"

ENTRANCE
HOLE = 1¼"
DIAMETER

11½" 10½"

LOCATE
WOOD FIN

FRONT (BACK SIMILAR)

4½"

SIDE

7½"

4½"

CUT WOOD BOTTOM
PIECE TO FIT
AFTER SIDES
ARE ASSEMBLED

LOCATE WOOD FIN

PLAN SECTION

#5
PARTS
DIAGRAM

5 TOOLS

Damp rag for glue drips
Drill
Drill bit for entrance hole
Hammer, screwdriver, or stapler
Nail set or countersink
Saw

SUPPLIES

Long finishing nails
Nails, screws, or wood staples
Pine cones
Used wood boards
Various sticks and a branch
Yellow wood glue

INSTRUCTIONS ———————

• Saw the flat pieces from the boards. Assemble the four sides with glue and fasteners. Attach the Roof flush to the Back. Drill the entrance hole. Saw the Bottom slightly smaller to make it easier to insert and to allow for drainage. Insert the Bottom into the birdhouse.

• Cut the branch to desired length and hold it in place on one Side of the birdhouse. Cut the bottom end of the branch at an angle so that it will sit flush against the wall or tree when you hang it. Attach this branch to the Side with screws or nails. This detail will create the illusion that the birdhouse grew as part of the tree.

• With glue and fasteners, place the Wood Fin piece onto the Front. Before attaching the sticks onto the Sides and Front, cut them to length and place them until you like the arrangement. If you just start attaching them you may run out of room by the time you get to the other side. If you own a band saw, you can carefully split the sticks down the center so that they lay flatter. Of course, round sticks will work just fine.

• Drill a small hole in the Back to hang this birdhouse on a wall. This is easier to do before you apply the pine cones onto the Front.

• Attach the pine cones with nails. This is easier to do if the pine cones are not too dry. Try to choose some that are fresh and won't fall apart. Long finishing nails work well for this. Once you have started them, use a nail set or countersink to drive the nails in farther. If you have trouble with this, you can also use wire to attach the pine cones onto the nails. Drive in a few nails that have heads and wrap the wire around the nails and pine cones.

• By choosing used boards with paint already on them, I avoided the painting step on this one. If you use painted boards, try to keep the fresh-cut edges on the back side so that they don't show. Of course, you can apply a bit of paint to your birdhouse. It works well on this style if you thin down latex paint and apply it like a stain so that the woodgrain shows through.

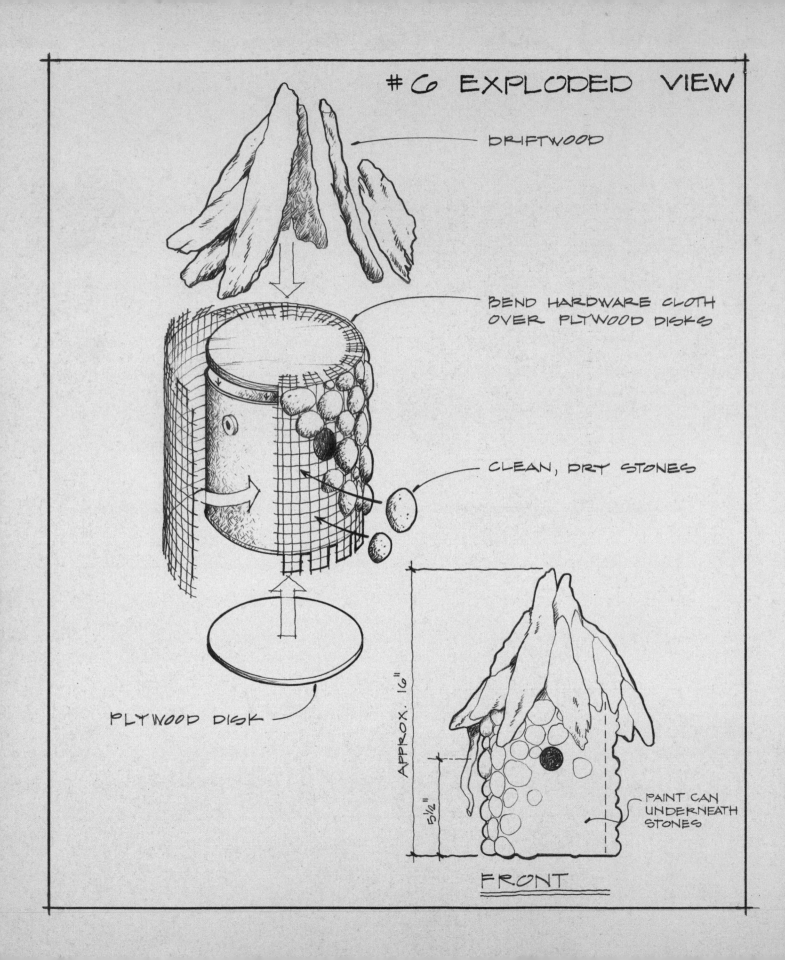

#6 EXPLODED VIEW

DRIFTWOOD

BEND HARDWARE CLOTH OVER PLYWOOD DISKS

CLEAN, DRY STONES

PLYWOOD DISK

APPROX. 16"

5½"

PAINT CAN UNDERNEATH STONES

FRONT

#6 PARTS DIAGRAM

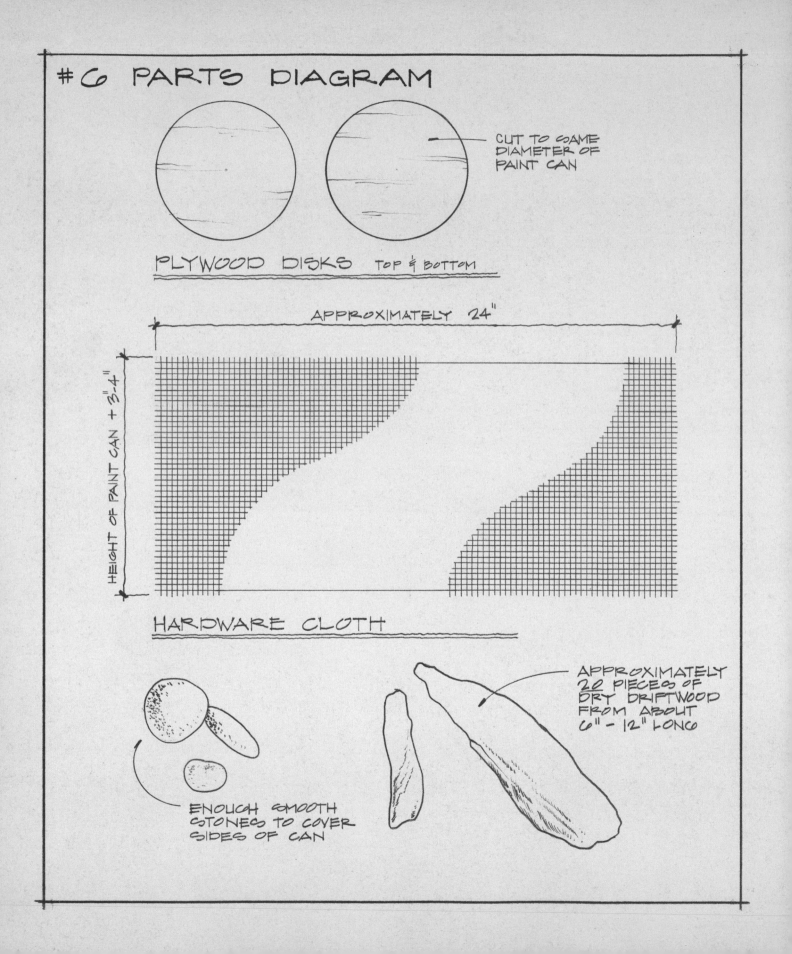

CUT TO SAME DIAMETER OF PAINT CAN

PLYWOOD DISKS TOP & BOTTOM

APPROXIMATELY 24"

HEIGHT OF PAINT CAN + 3"-4"

HARDWARE CLOTH

ENOUGH SMOOTH STONES TO COVER SIDES OF CAN

APPROXIMATELY 20 PIECES OF DRY DRIFTWOOD FROM ABOUT 6" - 12" LONG

6 TOOLS

Drill
Drill bit for metal for entrance
Hammer or stapler
Hot-glue gun and glue sticks
Metal snips
Pliers
Saw
Soft, clean cloth or diaper
Work gloves

SUPPLIES

Assorted clean, dry, smooth stones
Colored tile grout
Driftwood or sticks
Masking or electrical tape
Metal hardware cloth mesh
Nails or staples
One-gallon paint can
Plywood

INSTRUCTIONS ———————

• Begin with an empty, clean one-gallon paint can. Remove the handle, using pliers. Drill a hole in the can where you want the entrance hole, large enough to get the tip of the snips into. Draw the full size of the finished entrance hole on the face of the can around the hole you just drilled. Cut this hole as an "X" and then cut in the middle of each flap, using the snips. Work carefully, using the pliers to bend these tabs back on the outside face of the can. Set the paint can on the plywood as a template and trace around the bottom of the can twice. Saw these two Disks out. Set the can on top of one Disk and set the other Disk on top of the can. Tape these Disks to the can before the next step.

• Wearing work gloves, wrap the metal hardware cloth mesh around the can as snug as possible. Leave about an inch overhanging the top and bottom beyond the length of the can. Using the metal snips, cut the hardware cloth about every inch or so and bend it over to the plywood surface. Staple these flaps down to the plywood. Cut the hardware cloth at the entrance hole. Bend any loose wires back with pliers so there aren't sharp wires that will cut you or the birds.

• Lay the can on its side so that you are working on a horizontal surface. Apply a generous blob of hot glue to the back of each clean, dry stone and then quickly apply the stone to the hardware cloth so that the glue works its way into the mesh. Work very carefully so you don't burn yourself. The stones must be securely attached or you will have trouble with them coming off in the next step.

• Apply tile grout, following manufacturer's instructions. It is available in many colors from home improvement stores. Mix it to about the consistency of cake frosting and work it between the stones. Keep working with it as it dries, by rubbing off any excess with a soft damp cloth. (This part seems to go on forever.) Keep rinsing and wringing out your cloth as you go and finish with a clean dry cloth.

• Attach driftwood or sticks to the roof with hot glue and fasteners. While the hot glue won't hold up outdoors, it will hold the driftwood in place until you nail through into the top plywood Disk. Don't hammer too hard or you'll dislodge the stones. The color of the stones will be enhanced if you spray the birdhouse with a clear acrylic or varnish.

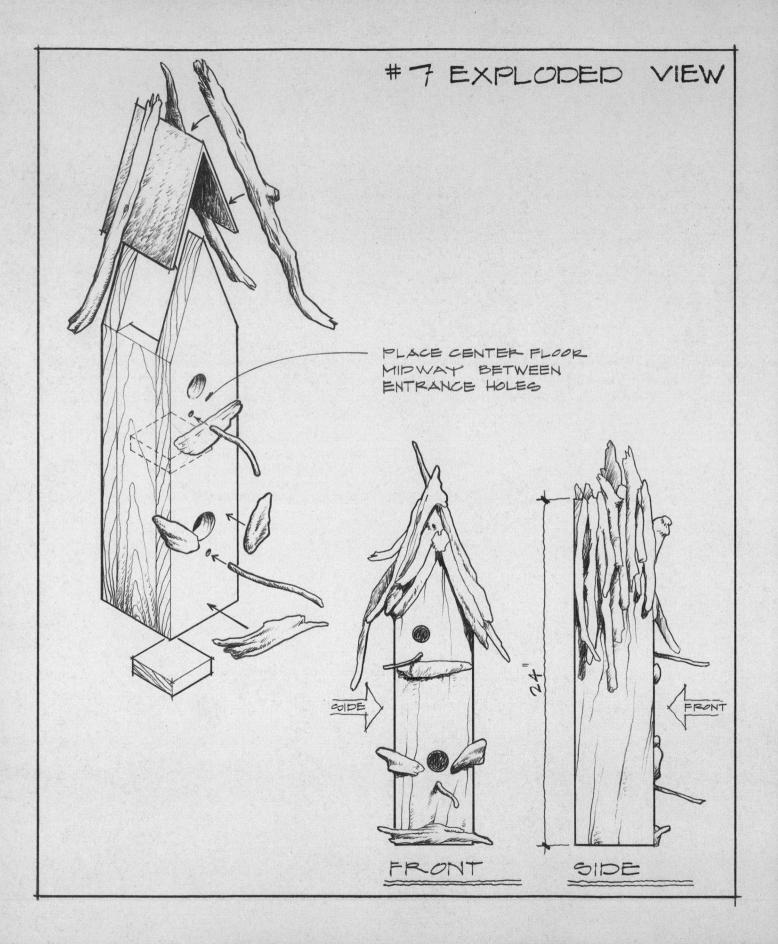

#7 EXPLODED VIEW

PLACE CENTER FLOOR
MIDWAY BETWEEN
ENTRANCE HOLES

SIDE

FRONT

24"

FRONT

SIDE

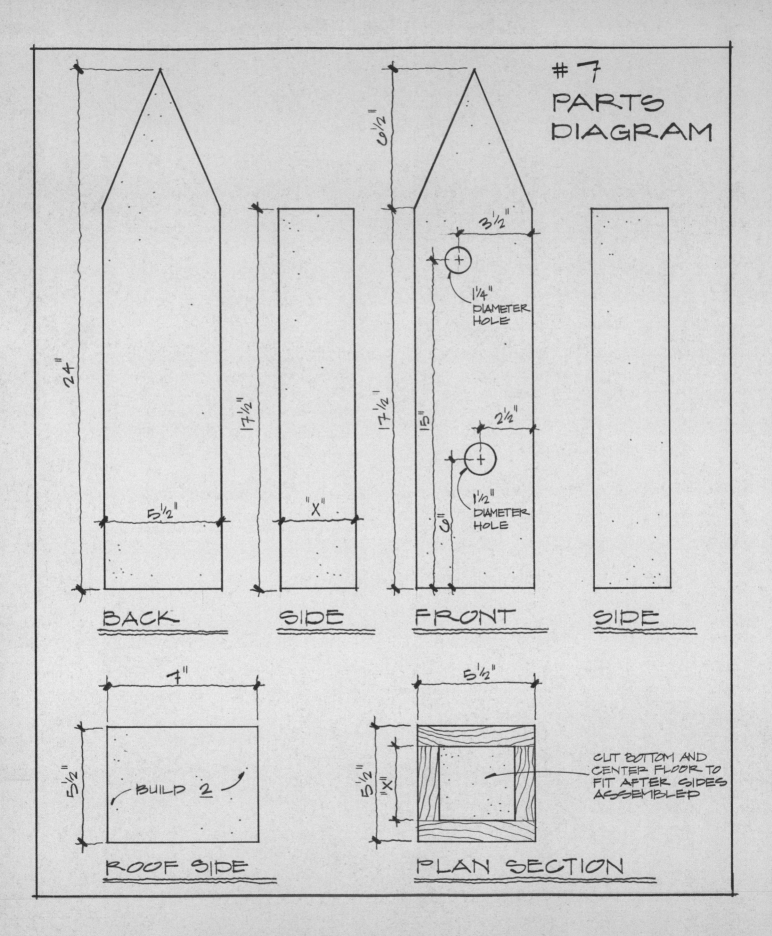

7
PARTS DIAGRAM

BACK

24"

5½"

SIDE

17½"

"X"

FRONT

9½"

3½"

1¼" DIAMETER HOLE

17½"

15"

2½"

1½" DIAMETER HOLE

9"

SIDE

ROOF SIDE

7"

5½"

BUILD 2

PLAN SECTION

5½"

5½"

"X"

CUT BOTTOM AND CENTER FLOOR TO FIT AFTER SIDES ASSEMBLED

7   TOOLS

Damp rag for glue drips
Drill
Drill bit for entrances and perches
Hammer, screwdriver, or stapler
Saw

SUPPLIES

Assorted driftwood pieces
Nails, screws, or wood staples
Rough wood boards
Yellow wood glue

INSTRUCTIONS

• Saw the flat pieces from the wood boards. If possible, choose a board with natural knot holes for the entrances. If not, drill the entrance holes on the Front now, or wait until it is built and drill them last.

• I find it easier to assemble the four sides first, overlapping the Back and Front over the two Sides. Apply glue to each joint as you assemble it. Keep a damp rag handy to wipe up glue drips while they are wet. Saw the Center Floor and Bottom. Insert these pieces into the birdhouse with glue and fasteners. Gaps around these pieces are desired as they help allow for drainage. Next, saw and attach the Roof Side pieces to the birdhouse.

• While I used driftwood for the roof and decoration of this birdhouse, you may choose to use sticks, branches, or some other material. I find it easiest when building a roof of this type to choose two or three main pieces to start with and decide how they look best. Once these are attached to the Roof Side pieces with nails, place smaller pieces of driftwood between the larger ones, filling all the gaps. I happened to find two small pieces of driftwood that resembled wings. These worked nicely on either side of the lower entrance hole on the Front.

• The perches can be driftwood, branches, or dowels. Hold them up to your structure to decide where they look best. If left a little long, they can add character. Drill holes for these. Apply a bit of glue before pushing them in. If they feel loose, try a bit larger perch. You may also want to hammer a small nail in at an angle through the perch into the Front of the birdhouse. If you choose to do this, it's less obvious if you drill a pilot hole first and nail it from the bottom.

The type and shape of the material you choose provides personality for your creation. I try to collect much more of these pieces than I think I'll need so that I am not limited in my possibilities. Keep your eyes open year-round. I have a very dear friend that collects a grocery bag full of driftwood every summer at her family beach cabin. You'll be surprised what friends will come up with when you spread the word that you are looking for unique building materials. Whether at the beach, the woods, or in a vacant lot in the city, there are materials out there just waiting to become part of one of your creations. Obviously, if these materials are found on property that is not your own, you should get permission first.

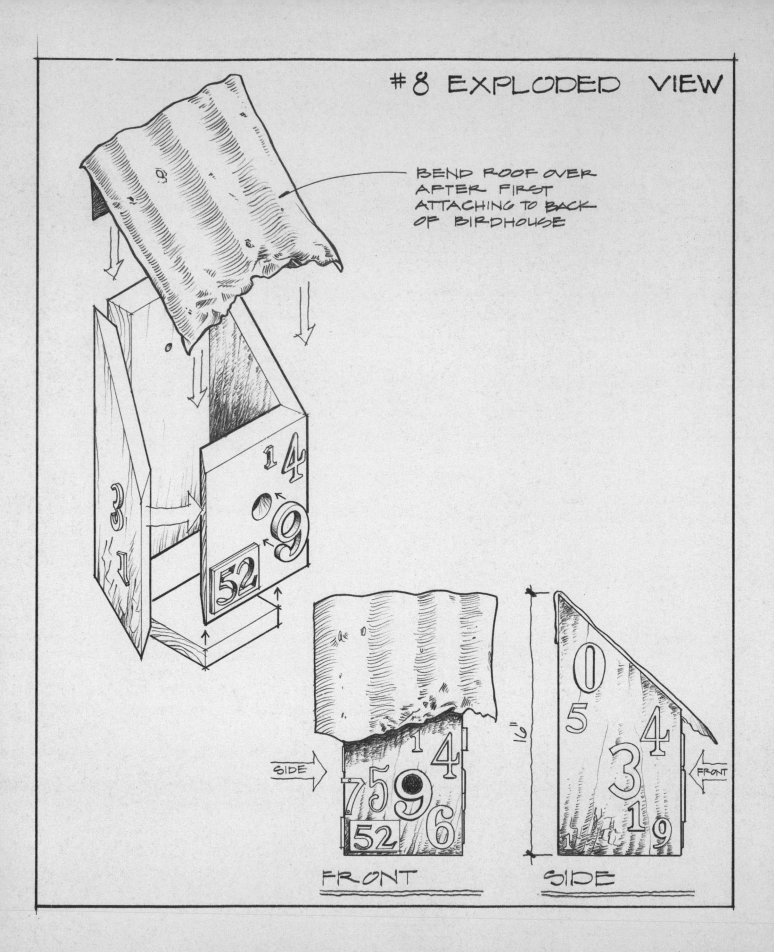

#8 EXPLODED VIEW

BEND ROOF OVER
AFTER FIRST
ATTACHING TO BACK
OF BIRDHOUSE

FRONT

SIDE

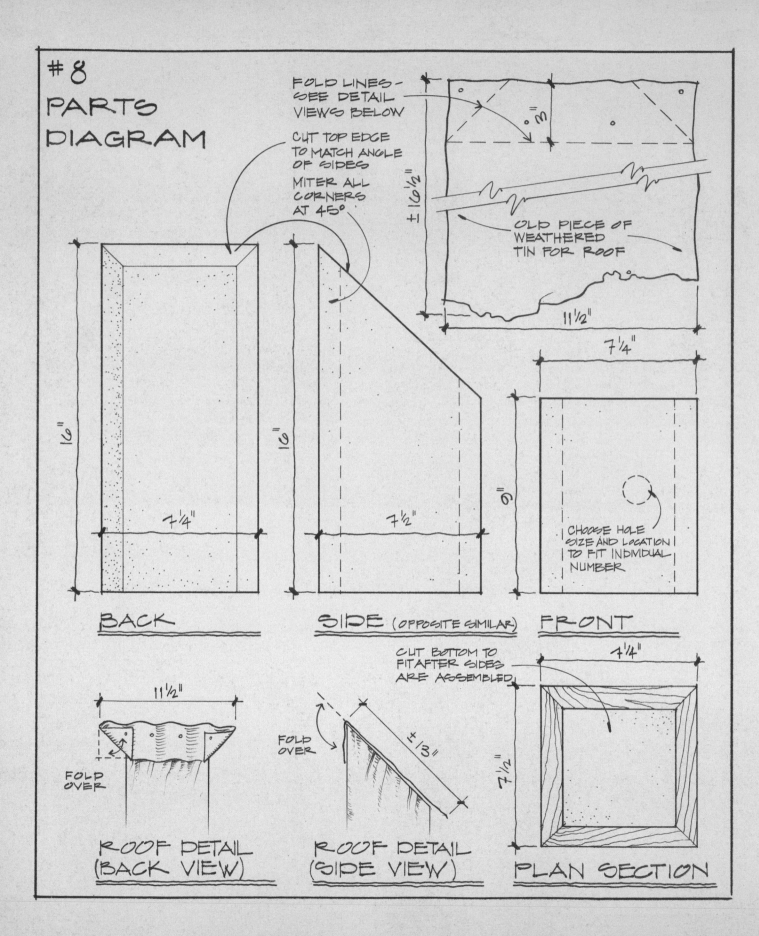

#8
PARTS
DIAGRAM

FOLD LINES—
SEE DETAIL
VIEWS BELOW

CUT TOP EDGE
TO MATCH ANGLE
OF SIDES

MITER ALL
CORNERS
AT 45°

± 9½"

3"

OLD PIECE OF
WEATHERED
TIN FOR ROOF

11½"

16"

16"

7¼"

BACK

7¼"

SIDE (OPPOSITE SIMILAR)

7½"

FRONT

7¼"

16"

CHOOSE HOLE
SIZE AND LOCATION
TO FIT INDIVIDUAL
NUMBER

FOLD
OVER

11½"

ROOF DETAIL
(BACK VIEW)

CUT BOTTOM TO
FIT AFTER SIDES
ARE ASSEMBLED

FOLD
OVER

± 13"

ROOF DETAIL
(SIDE VIEW)

7¼"

7½"

PLAN SECTION

TOOLS

Damp rag for glue drips
Drill
Drill bit for entrance
Hammer, screwdriver, or stapler
Jigsaw with metal blade or tin snips
Saw

SUPPLIES

Assorted house numbers
Brass and copper spray paints
Corrugated metal
Nails, screws, or wood staples
Rough wood boards
Yellow wood glue

INSTRUCTIONS ————————————

• Saw the flat pieces from the wood boards. I mitered the corners to minimize the side seams. Apply glue to each joint as you assemble it. Keep a damp rag handy to wipe up glue drips while they are wet. Attach the Back to the Sides and then attach the Front. I like to start with the Back first because it gives you a chance to get used to how the wood reacts to the fasteners you've chosen. If you want to hang this one on a wall, drill a small hole in the Back.

• If the sides don't go together square (which is common with old wood), straighten the four corners by gently pushing or hammering it square while the glue is still wet. Once the four sides are together, insert the Bottom piece. If you want the Bottom removable for cleaning, use screws and no glue to attach it. Saw the Bottom slightly smaller to help it go in easier. The cracks that are left where it meets the sides allow for drainage once you put it to use outside. For additional drainage, you may want to drill a couple of ¼" holes in the Bottom.

• The Roof for this particular birdhouse is a great piece of rusted corrugated metal. This type of sheet metal can be cut, using a metal blade in a jigsaw or with a pair of tin snips. If you use the saw method, take care to anchor the metal well to your work surface. This kind of cutting can create quite a vibration.

• To attach the Roof, predrill four holes in the metal along what will become the back flap. Then place the birdhouse face down on your work surface and center the Roof material across the back of the birdhouse. Screw in the four screws. Stand the birdhouse up and bend the Roof forward, using your hands. At first it won't want to stay all the way down. Using a hammer, strike the metal along the top ridge to bend it sharper. Go easy at first as bending around a corner will flatten out the corrugations. I didn't use fasteners on the front of the roof.

• I collected a variety of numbers from hardware stores, antiques stores, and thrift stores. Some are plastic, others are metal. I painted some with copper and brass spray paint before attaching them. Using a couple of colors on the same piece will give it an aged appearance and add to the beauty that the weathered boards had to begin with.

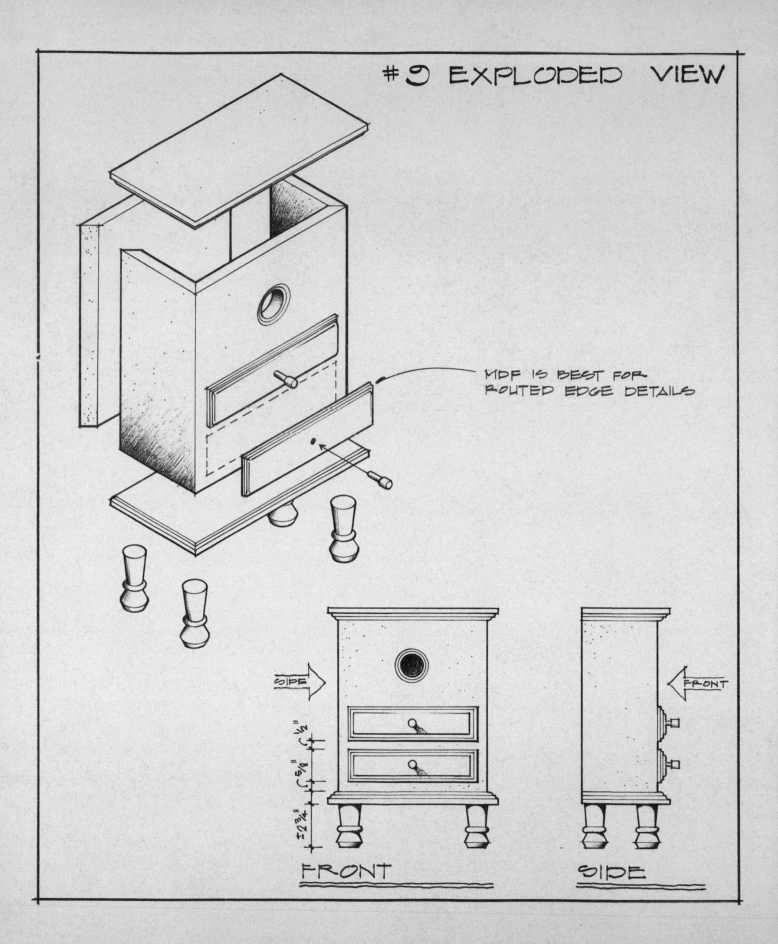

#9 EXPLODED VIEW

MDF IS BEST FOR ROUTED EDGE DETAILS

SIDE ⟹

½"

⅝"

±2¾"

⟸ FRONT

FRONT

SIDE

Birds of a Feather

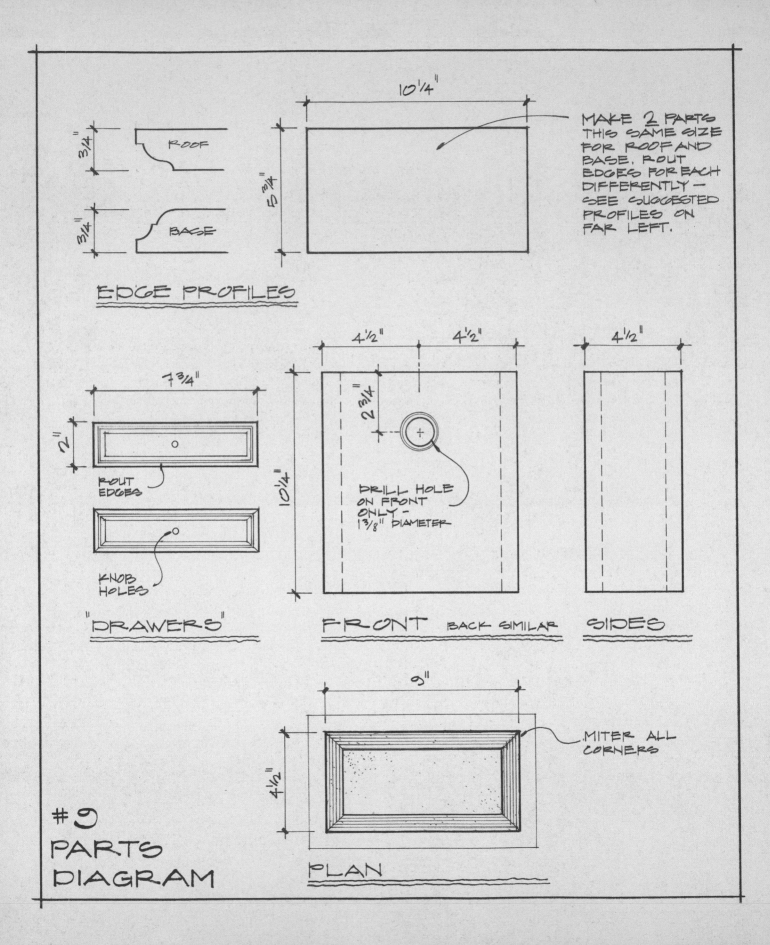

EDGE PROFILES

ROOF
3/4"

BASE
3/4"

10 1/4"

5 3/4"

MAKE 2 PARTS THIS SAME SIZE FOR ROOF AND BASE. ROUT EDGES FOR EACH DIFFERENTLY — SEE SUGGESTED PROFILES ON FAR LEFT.

"DRAWERS"

7 3/4"

2"

ROUT EDGES

KNOB HOLES

FRONT BACK SIMILAR

4 1/2" 4 1/2"

2 3/4"

10 1/4"

DRILL HOLE ON FRONT ONLY - 1 3/8" DIAMETER

SIDES

4 1/2"

#9
PARTS
DIAGRAM

PLAN

9"

4 1/2"

MITER ALL CORNERS

9   TOOLS

Damp rag for glue drips
Drill
Drill bit for entrance hole
Hammer, screwdriver, or stapler
Router with bit
Sandpaper
Saw

SUPPLIES

Clear matte acrylic spray paint
Latex paint
MDF or Plywood
Nails, screws, or wood staples
Turned wood for legs
Wood putty or spackle
Yellow wood glue

INSTRUCTIONS ———————————

• Saw the flat pieces from the sheet material. If you use MDF, you will have less trouble cleaning up the edges before you paint (as plywood leaves an exposed grain along the cut edge). The best way to build this birdhouse is to miter all four vertical sides. However, you can also just build a box with overlapped corners. Apply yellow glue to each joint as you assemble it. Keep a damp rag handy to wipe up glue drips while they are wet. Putty the holes and sand before painting.

• Drill the entrance hole in the Front, using a 1⅛" bit, and then finish the edge with a contoured router bit. If you are going to rout the entrance, do it before attaching the Side, Roof, Base, or Drawers so that you have a flat surface on which to rest the router. The Roof, Base, and Drawers are also routed to achieve the edge detail. I shaped these pieces prior to assembly by clamping or screwing the parts to my workbench to hold them while I routed the contoured edge. Use caution when using a power tool, such as a router, particularly when working with small parts such as these. If you want to be really fancy, and you have more patience than I do, you could make the "drawers" actually work.

• The legs are some wood turnings that I found at a store that sold woodworker's supplies. You can also cut up some old wooden candle holders, or cut down some short turned table legs that are readily available at home improvement stores. Attach the legs to the bottom of the Base by screwing or nailing them on from the top of the Base prior to attaching it to the sides of the birdhouse. If it doesn't sit level, sand the longer leg(s) until the Base doesn't wobble.

• Although the paint technique is relatively simple, it may require some practice. Paint each of the parts with latex paint. Vary the colors per part. The woodgrain effect was achieved using colored pencils once the paint is dry. Observe obvious woodgrain on a piece of real wood as a guide. Use short strokes. This part takes some time, but your patience will pay off. Apply a clear acrylic spray paint to preserve the surface. I found the other two wooden boxes at a home decorating store and then painted them all the same.

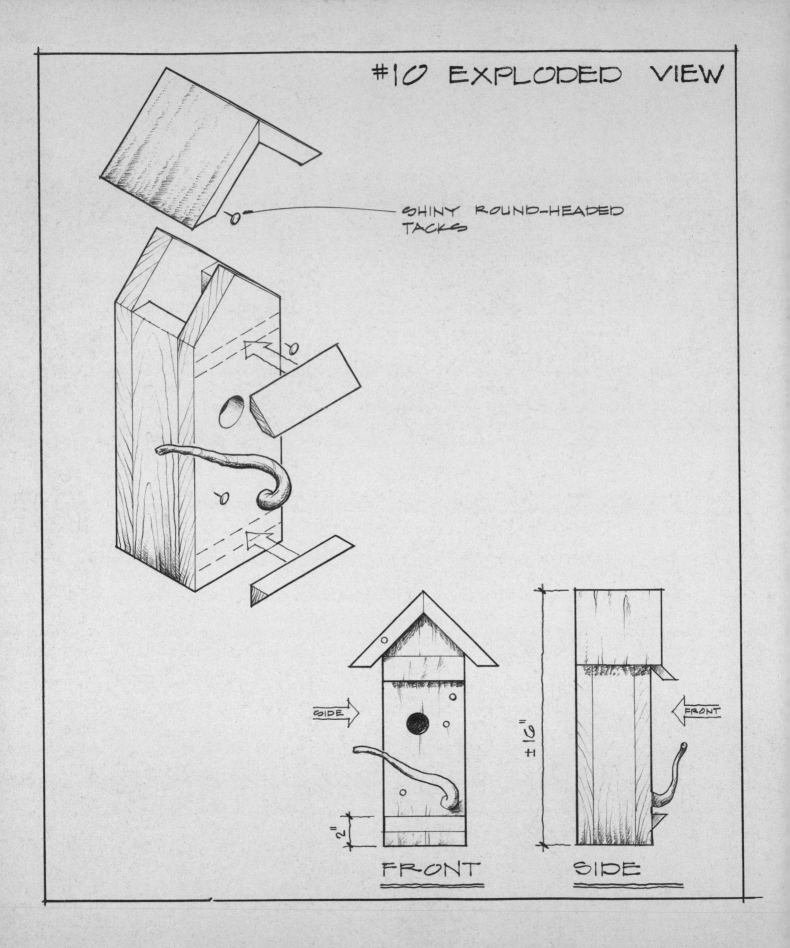

#10 EXPLODED VIEW

SHINY ROUND-HEADED TACKS

FRONT

SIDE

±16"

2"

SIDE

FRONT

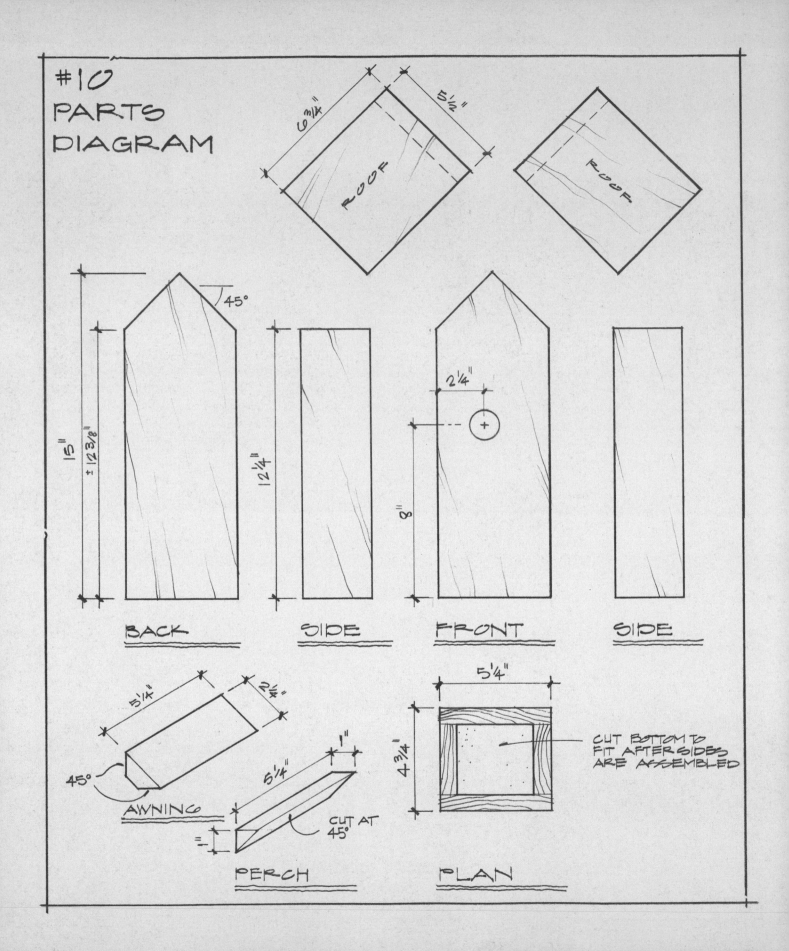

#10
PARTS
DIAGRAM

ROOF

6³/₄" 5¹/₂"

ROOF

45°

15" ± 12³/₈"

12¹/₄"

2¹/₄"

8"

BACK

SIDE

FRONT

SIDE

5¹/₄" 2¹/₄"

45°

AWNING

1"

5¹/₄"

1"

CUT AT 45°

PERCH

5¹/₄"

4³/₄"

CUT BOTTOM TO
FIT AFTER SIDES
ARE ASSEMBLED

PLAN

10 TOOLS

Damp rag for glue drips
Drill
Drill bit for entrance hole
Hammer, screwdriver, or stapler
Saw

SUPPLIES

Black latex paint
Branch
Clear matte acrylic spray paint
Nails, screws, or wood staples
Oil pastels
Round-headed nails or tacks
Wood boards
Yellow wood glue

INSTRUCTIONS ————————————

• Saw the flat pieces from the wood boards. Miter the Roof ends as indicated. Assemble the four sides. Use finishing nails (a nail with little or no head) if you don't want the nail holes to be obvious. Apply yellow glue to each joint as you assemble it. Keep a damp rag handy to wipe up glue drips while they are wet. Insert the bottom piece into the birdhouse and nail or screw it in place—don't use glue if you want it to be removable.

• Attach the Roof pieces. The Roof should sit flush with the Back. Drill a hole in the Back if you wish to hang the birdhouse. Once the Roof is on you can attach the Awning and Perch pieces onto the Front. You can achieve different looks for this style birdhouse, depending on how far apart you place these pieces.

• I think it is best to attach the Perch prior to drilling the entrance hole. The branch I used had a bend in it right where it attached to the birdhouse, so I drilled a hole the same size as the branch and just glued it in place. If you wish to use a finishing nail, it is best to drill a small pilot hole through the branch once it is in place so you don't split it. This would be a good time to fill the nail holes, if desired. Sand lightly if needed, but don't sand the woodgrain smooth.

• Although the paint technique on this particular birdhouse is relatively simple, it may require some practice. Paint the whole structure with black latex paint. Then, using the oil pastels, apply the color to the surface. If you use strokes across the grain it will help accentuate it. Remember, if you don't like it, you can always start over and paint it again. Work with different colors to see what different effects you can achieve. This part takes some time, but your patience will pay off. Apply a clear acrylic spray paint to preserve the surface.

• I hammered in round headed nails found at a home improvement store for additional detail. Applied to appear randomly, they almost look like stars.

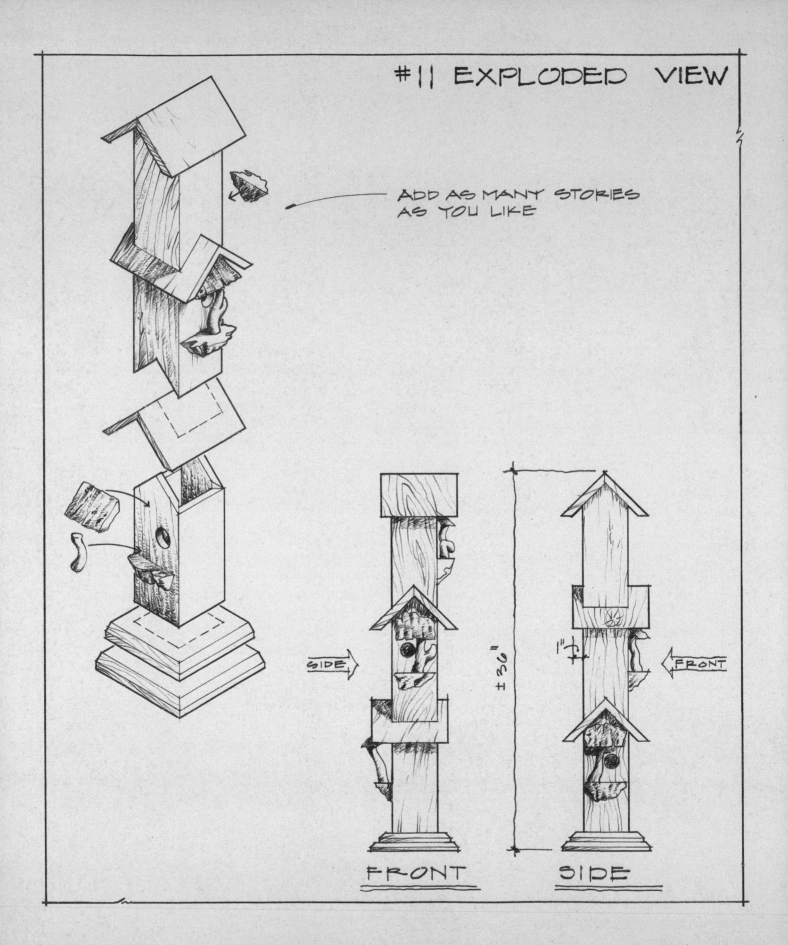

#11 EXPLODED VIEW

ADD AS MANY STORIES
AS YOU LIKE

SIDE

±36"

1"

FRONT

FRONT

SIDE

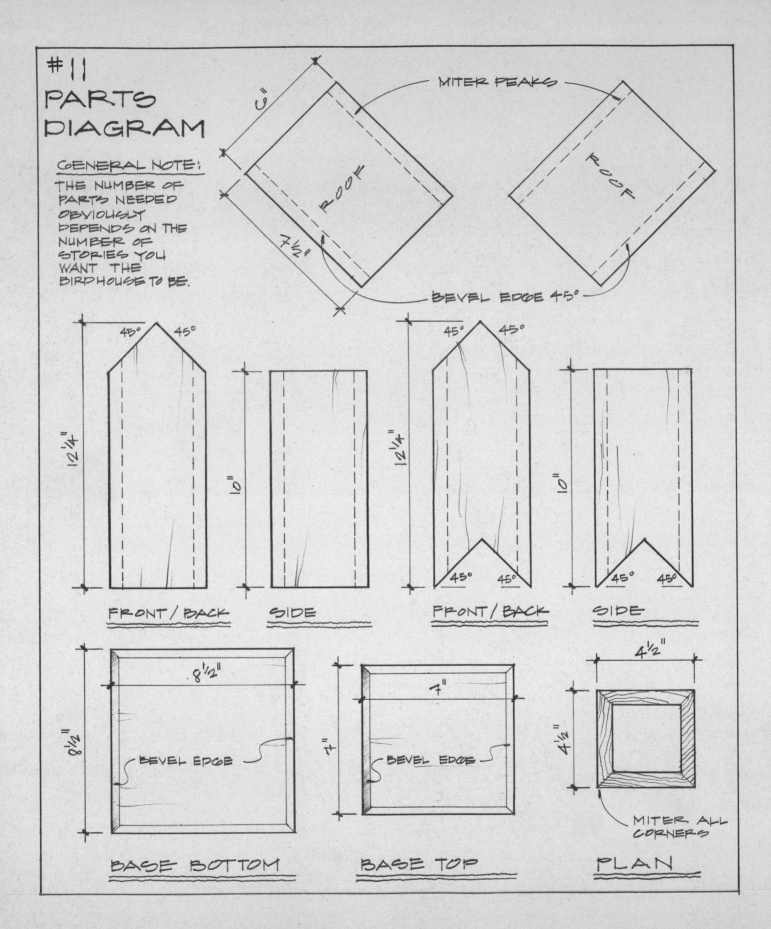

#11
PARTS
DIAGRAM

GENERAL NOTE:
THE NUMBER OF
PARTS NEEDED
OBVIOUSLY
DEPENDS ON THE
NUMBER OF
STORIES YOU
WANT THE
BIRDHOUSE TO BE.

MITER PEAKS

ROOF

ROOF

6"

7½"

BEVEL EDGE 45°

45° 45°

12¼"

10"

FRONT/BACK   SIDE

45° 45°

12¼"

10"

45° 45°

45° 45°

FRONT/BACK   SIDE

8½"

8½"

BEVEL EDGE

BASE BOTTOM

7"

7"

BEVEL EDGE

BASE TOP

4½"

4½"

MITER ALL
CORNERS

PLAN

TOOLS

Damp rag for glue drips
Drill
Drill bit for entrance hole
Hammer, screwdriver, or stapler
Newspaper
Saw

SUPPLIES

Bark pieces
Branch
Black latex paint
Clear matte acrylic spray paint
Flat-headed nails or tacks
Light colored latex or acrylic paint
Nails, screws, or wood staples
Wood boards
Yellow wood glue

INSTRUCTIONS

This birdhouse is essentially the same house stacked three tall. If you look at the gallery photo on page 6, you will see a seven story one where my wife thinks I went a little out of control. You can use these instructions to make one with as many stories as you see fit.

• Saw the flat pieces from the the wood boards. Miter the ends as indicated. The top two stories have notches in them that match the angle of the roof of the level below. Assemble the four sides of each level. Use finishing nails (nails with little or no head) if you don't want the nail holes to be obvious. Apply glue to each joint as you assemble it. Keep a damp rag handy to wipe up glue drips while they are wet.

• Attach the Roof pieces. Once the Roof is on you can attach the awnings and perches onto the Front pieces. You can achieve different looks for this style birdhouse, depending on how far apart you place these pieces. I used portions of bark cut from a medium sized log. The perches are curly willow branches. I think it is best to attach the perch prior to drilling the entrance hole. If you wish to use a finishing nail, it is best to drill a small pilot hole through the branch once it is in place so you don't split it. This would be a good time to fill the nail holes, if desired. Sand lightly if needed, but don't sand the woodgrain smooth.

• Although the paint technique is relatively simple, it may require some practice. Paint the whole structure with flat black latex paint. Then, using other lighter colors of latex or acrylic paint, apply the color to the surface. The technique I used is called dry brushing. Dip the brush into the paint, but then use it on a piece of newspaper first to use up most of the paint on the brush. Next, lightly paint the surface, using strokes across the grain to help accentuate it. Remember, if you don't like it you can always start over and paint it again.

• Apply a clear acrylic spray paint to preserve the surface. I hammered in flat-headed tacks for additional detail. Applied to appear randomly, they almost look like stars.

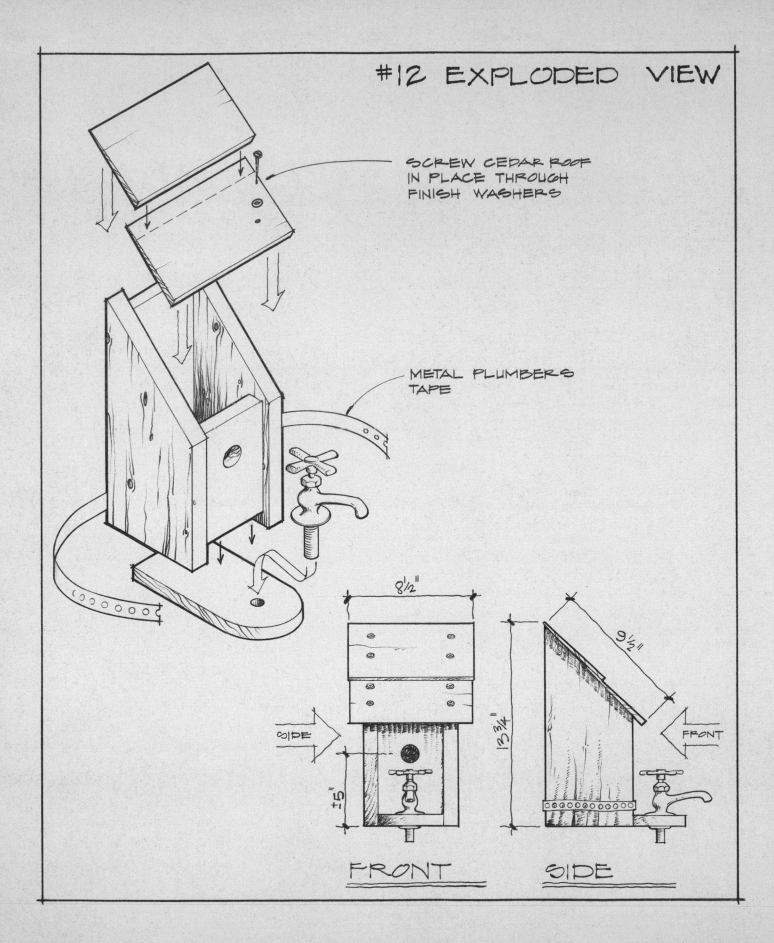

#12 EXPLODED VIEW

SCREW CEDAR ROOF
IN PLACE THROUGH
FINISH WASHERS

METAL PLUMBERS
TAPE

8½"

9½"

13¾"

±5"

SIDE

FRONT

FRONT

SIDE

Bird Bath

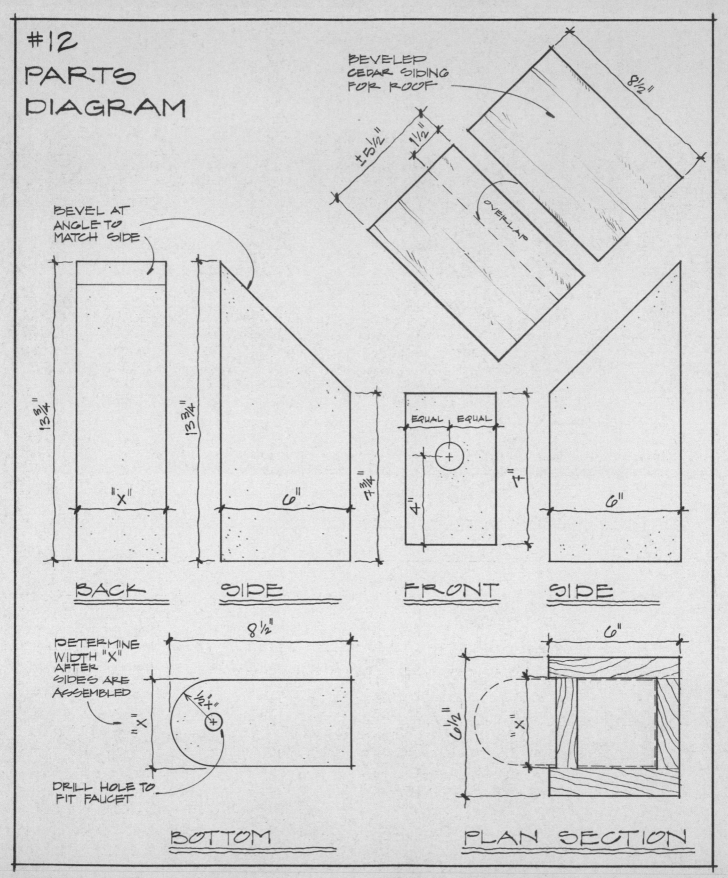

#12
PARTS
DIAGRAM

BEVELED
CEDAR SIDING
FOR ROOF

8½"

± 5½"   1½"

OVERLAP

BEVEL AT
ANGLE TO
MATCH SIDE

13⅝"

13¾"

"X"

BACK

13¾"

6"

7¾"

SIDE

EQUAL   EQUAL

4"

7"

FRONT

6"

SIDE

DETERMINE
WIDTH "X"
AFTER
SIDES ARE
ASSEMBLED

8½"

½"

"X"

DRILL HOLE TO
FIT FAUCET

BOTTOM

6"

6½"

"X"

PLAN SECTION

12 TOOLS

Damp rag for glue drips
Drill
Drill bit for entrance hole
Hammer, screwdriver, or stapler
Saw

SUPPLIES

Beveled cedar siding
Faucet
Finish washers
Metal plumbers tape
Nails, screws, or wood staples
Rough wood boards
Yellow wood glue

INSTRUCTIONS

- Saw the flat pieces from the wood boards. If you can, choose a board with a natural knot hole for the entrance. If not, drill the entrance hole on the Front now, or wait until it is built and drill it last.

- Assemble the four sides first. On this particular birdhouse I overlapped the Sides over the Front and Back pieces, insetting the Front slightly. Apply glue to each joint as you assemble it. Keep a damp rag handy to wipe up glue drips while they are wet. I like to start with the back first because it gives you a chance to get used to how the wood reacts to the fasteners you've chosen.

- This is a good time to drill a small hole in the Back near the top if you are going to want to hang the birdhouse.

- Attach the faucet by drilling a hole in the Bottom to accept the faucet's threaded flange. I drilled the hole slightly smaller and then screwed the faucet into the hole before attaching the Bottom to the birdhouse.

- If the four sides don't go together square (which is common with old wood), take this opportunity to straighten the four corners by gently pushing or hammering it square while the glue is still wet. Insert the Bottom. If you want the Bottom removable for cleaning, use screws and no glue to attach it. For additional drainage, you may want to drill a couple of ¼" holes in the base.

- Next add the Roof pieces. I used pieces of beveled cedar siding. Attach these pieces, using screws with finish washers. Finish washers are shaped to fit around the head of a screw.

- Wrap and screw a strap of plumbers tape around the bottom of the outside of the birdhouse where it can naturally weather to a rich rust finish over time. This is a very good example of a unique birdhouse that can be constructed entirely out of recycled materials.

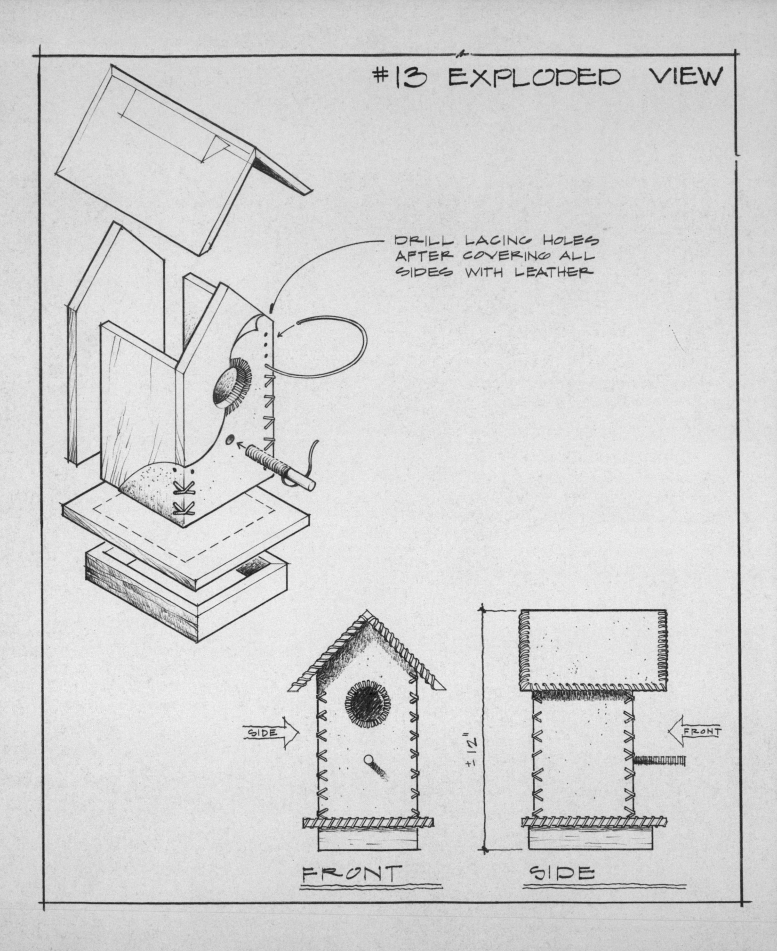

#13 EXPLODED VIEW

DRILL LACING HOLES
AFTER COVERING ALL
SIDES WITH LEATHER

SIDE →

± 12"

← FRONT

FRONT

SIDE

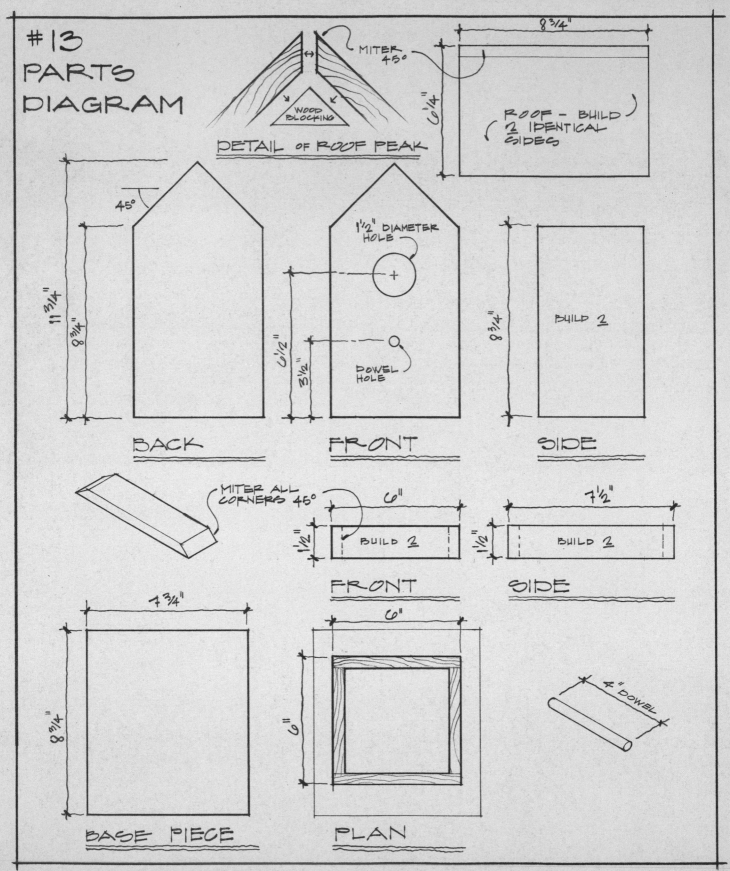

13
PARTS
DIAGRAM

DETAIL OF ROOF PEAK

MITER 45°

WOOD BLOCKING

8 3/4"

6 1/4"

ROOF - BUILD 2 IDENTICAL SIDES

45°

BACK

11 3/4"

8 1/4"

1 1/2" DIAMETER HOLE

DOWEL HOLE

FRONT

6 1/2"

3 1/2"

SIDE

BUILD 2

8 3/4"

MITER ALL CORNERS 45°

6"

1 1/2"

BUILD 2

FRONT

7 1/2"

1 1/2"

BUILD 2

SIDE

7 3/4"

8 3/4"

BASE PIECE

6"

6"

PLAN

4" DOWEL

13 TOOLS

- Damp rag for glue drips
- Drill
- Drill bits for entrance and perches
- Drill bit for lace holes
- Hammer, screwdriver, or stapler
- Newspaper
- Saw
- Scissors or razor blade

SUPPLIES

- Clear leather finish
- Leather
- Leather lacing
- Nails, screws, or wood staples
- ½" or ¾" plywood
- Spray adhesive
- ½" wooden dowel (4")
- Yellow wood glue or hot glue

INSTRUCTIONS

- Saw the flat pieces from plywood. Drill the entrance and perch holes in the Front now. Drill the perch hole slightly larger to fit the dowel when it is wrapped with lacing. It is easier to do this before you assemble the four sides. Assemble the four sides, using fasteners and glue. Attach the Roof pieces to each other, placing the wood blocking inside the peak. Keep the Roof and the Base separate from the sides until after the leather is applied. Lay the leather out flat, face down. Cut a piece long enough to wrap around the four sides with enough left for a 2" overlap. Cut pieces large enough to cover the top of the Roof and Base with about 3" extra all the way around. Soft, thin leather works best.

- Spread the leather cut for the sides face down on some newspaper. Evenly spray the back of the piece of leather with spray adhesive. Leaving about 1" of overhang along one edge where the side and back meet and along the top and bottom edges, lay the birdhouse onto the leather. Wrap the leather around it as if you are wrapping a present. Pull the leather gently at each edge as you go to keep it smooth. On the back edge, fold the overhang onto the Back of the birdhouse, and lay the other end of the leather over this flap. You may need to apply extra adhesive along the edge where they overlap. Trim the excess leather away along the overlap. Fold the extra at the top and bottom to the inside. Cover the Base and Roof, using the same steps, leaving enough of the flaps on all sides to wrap under and adhere to the underside.

- Drill lacing holes on the corner edges of all four sides, the Roof, and the Base. Drill holes around the entrance hole. Use a drill bit larger than the lacing or you will be frustrated trying to get the lacing through the holes. Cut the end of the lacing at an angle to act as a needle. Start at one end and lace your way around each part. I laced the four walls like shoe laces, crisscrossing as I went. Glue the ends of the lacing with hot glue if needed. Cut the leather away from the perch hole. Wrap the perch with lacing and glue with hot glue. After the lacing is complete, you can assemble all the parts, using hot glue or yellow wood glue, taking care not to drip on the leather. Keep a damp rag handy to wipe up glue drips while they are wet. Once the birdhouse is assembled, apply a clear leather finish to give it an aged look and protect the leather.

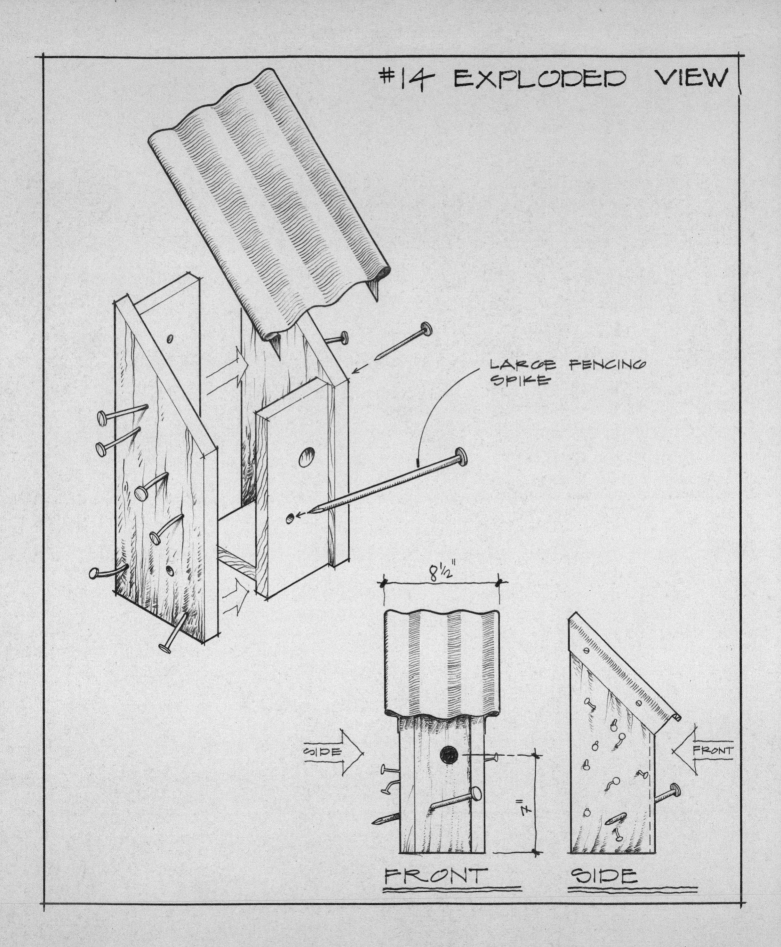

#14 EXPLODED VIEW

LARGE FENCING SPIKE

8½"

7"

SIDE

FRONT

FRONT   **SIDE**

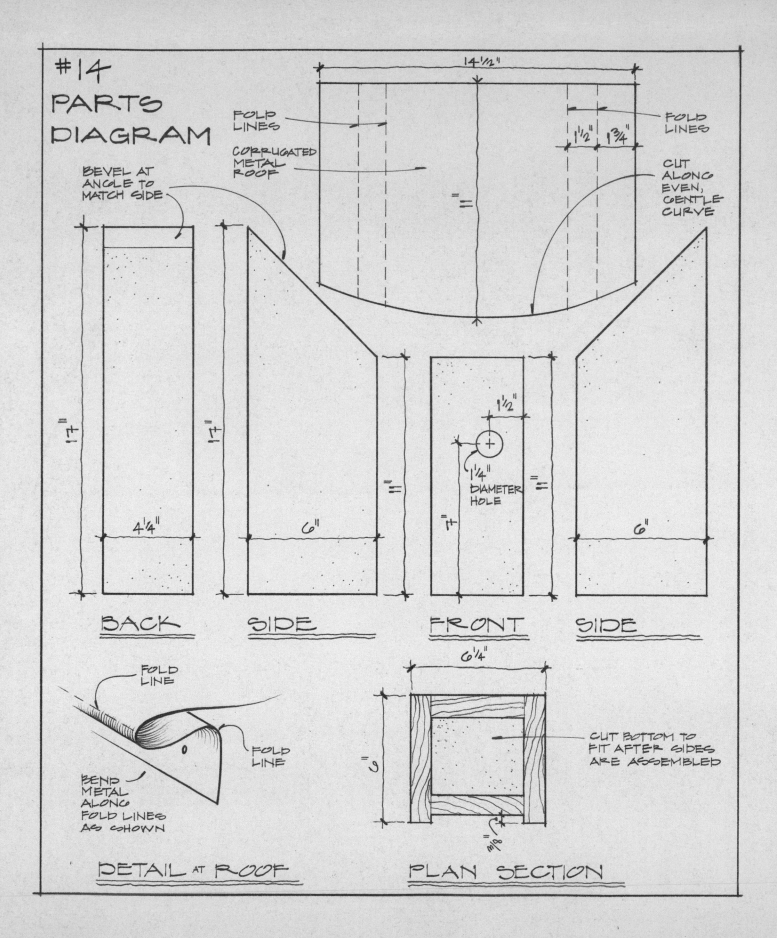

#14
PARTS
DIAGRAM

14½"

FOLD LINES

CORRUGATED METAL ROOF

1½" 1¾"

FOLD LINES

CUT ALONG EVEN, GENTLE CURVE

BEVEL AT ANGLE TO MATCH SIDE

17"

4¼"

BACK

17"

6"

SIDE

1½"

1¼" DIAMETER HOLE

FRONT

6"

SIDE

FOLD LINE

FOLD LINE

BEND METAL ALONG FOLD LINES AS SHOWN

DETAIL at ROOF

6¼"

9"

⅜"

CUT BOTTOM TO FIT AFTER SIDES ARE ASSEMBLED

PLAN SECTION

14 TOOLS

Damp rag for glue drips
Drill
Drill bit for entrance hole
Hammer, screwdriver, or stapler
Jigsaw with metal blade or tin snips
Saw

SUPPLIES

Corrugated metal
Large fence spike and nails
Nails, screws, or wood staples
Rough wood boards
Yellow wood glue

INSTRUCTIONS

• Saw the flat pieces from the wood boards. Assemble the four sides first, overlapping the two Sides to the Back. Apply yellow glue to each joint as you assemble it. Keep a damp rag handy to wipe up glue drips while they are wet. Then attach the Front. I like to start with the Back first because it gives you a chance to get used to how the wood reacts to the fasteners you've chosen. If you want to hang this one on a wall, drill a small hole in the Back.

• If the sides don't go together square (which is common with old wood), straighten the four corners by gently pushing or hammering it square while the glue is still wet. Once the four sides are together, the Bottom can be inserted. If you want the Bottom removable for cleaning, use screws and no glue to attach it. Saw the Bottom slightly smaller to help it go in easier. The cracks that are left where it meets the sides allow for drainage once you put it to use outside. For additional drainage, you may want to drill a couple of ¼" holes in the bottom.

• The Roof for this particular birdhouse is a piece of corrugated metal. This type of sheet metal can be cut, using a metal blade in a jigsaw or with a pair of tin snips. If you use the saw method, be careful to anchor the metal well to your work surface. This kind of cutting can create quite a vibration.

• Bend the sides of the Roof to fit over the sides of the birdhouse. You'll achieve a straighter bend if you use the edge of a workbench or board as a guide. Bend it too far and then pull it apart enough to get it over the sides. Drill pilot holes for the screws you use to hold the Roof on.

• Drill a hole at an angle through one corner of the Front of the birdhouse for the large spike. You can find these large spikes at a home improvement store. Hammer assorted nails into both sides of the birdhouse bending a few as you go.

• This type of birdhouse will weather naturally if exposed to the elements. Try not to use galvanized nails, as they are not meant to rust. The roof material, if galvanized, will maintain its shine for many seasons.

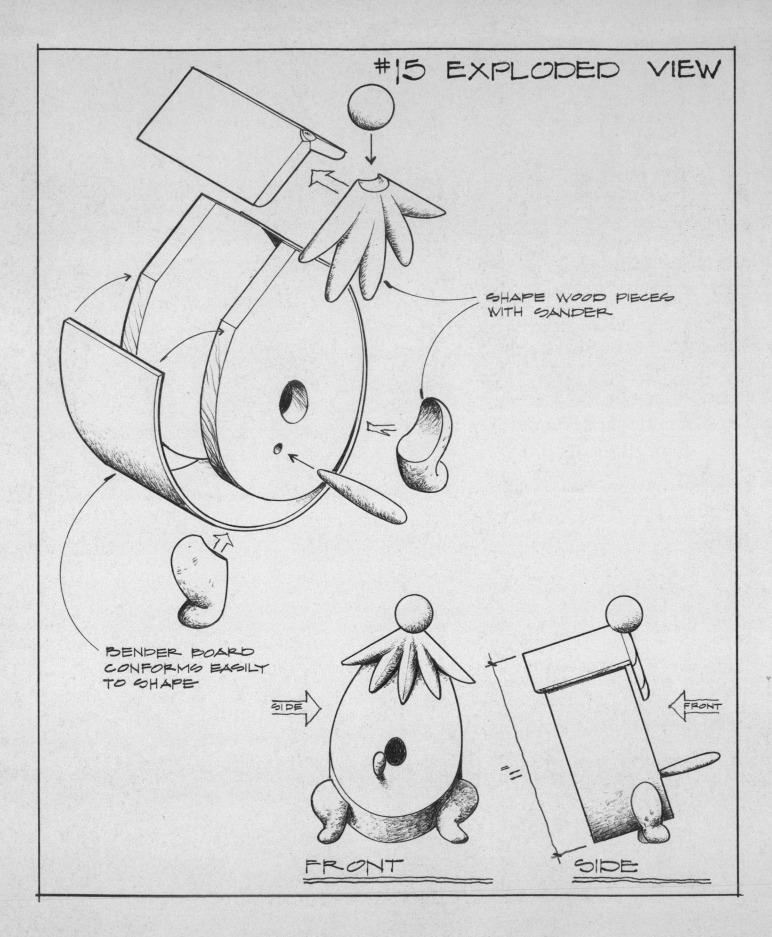

15 EXPLODED VIEW

SHAPE WOOD PIECES
WITH SANDER

BENDER BOARD
CONFORMS EASILY
TO SHAPE

SIDE

FRONT

FRONT

SIDE

#15 PARTS DIAGRAM

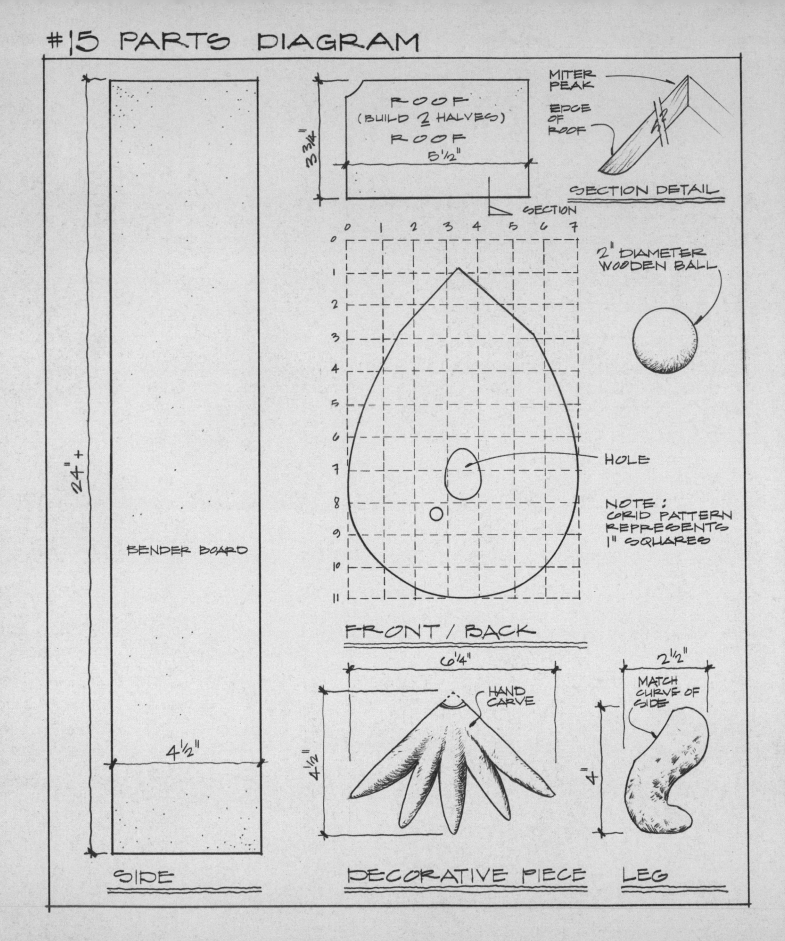

24"+

BENDER BOARD

4½"

SIDE

ROOF
(BUILD 2 HALVES)
ROOF
5½"
3¾"

SECTION

MITER PEAK
EDGE OF ROOF
½"

SECTION DETAIL

2" DIAMETER WOODEN BALL

HOLE

NOTE:
GRID PATTERN REPRESENTS 1" SQUARES

0 1 2 3 4 5 6 7
0
1
2
3
4
5
6
7
8
9
10
11

FRONT / BACK

6'4"

HAND CARVE

4½"

DECORATIVE PIECE

2½"

MATCH CURVE OF SIDE

4"

LEG

15 TOOLS

Clamp
Damp rag for glue drips ·
Drill
Drill bit for entrance and perch
Hammer, screwdriver, or stapler
Sander or sandpaper
Sanding disk or wheel
Saw

SUPPLIES

Bender board
Latex paint
MDF or plywood
Nails, screws, or wood staples
Spray paint
Wood putty or spackle
Wooden ball
¾" wooden dowel
Yellow wood glue

INSTRUCTIONS ————————

• Saw the Front and Back pieces from the sheet material. A jigsaw or band saw works best. If you would like the entrance hole to be egg shaped, predrill a hole and then saw it to shape.

• Saw the sides from one long strip of bender board. Bender board is a type of thin plywood that is manufactured to bend around curves. To find it, try a lumber store or look in the business section of the telephone directory under plywood. Assemble the birdhouse by starting at one end and wrapping bender board around the edges of Front and Back pieces, applying glue and fasteners as you go. Once this is done, trim the excess off the other end. Fill any gaps or edge grain that shows around the Front edge with wood putty. Sand these areas smooth. An electric sander will work best here, but, with a bit more elbow grease, sandpaper wrapped around a wood block will also work.

• Saw the Decorative Piece and the Legs out of MDF. If you want legs as thick as the ones in the photograph, laminate two pieces together for each, using glue and a clamp until dry. I "carved" the shapes, using a sanding disk. These are available in a hand-held model or use a bench mounted sanding wheel. Use great care to hold the part as you are sanding. Saw the profile from the MDF, using a jigsaw or band saw, and then round it, using the sander. Saw or sand the legs to match the contour of the curve where they will be attached. Sand the dowel to shape for the perch. These parts can also be carved or whittled with a knife if you know how. Assemble the Roof sides to the Front with glue and fasteners. Once these are together, drill a pilot hole through and sand a flat spot on the front of the Roof peak. Attach the wooden ball, using a screw from the inside.

• I painted all of the parts before I assembled them so that I didn't have to mask anything. Paint all parts with two or more coats of latex paint, sanding lightly between coats. The mottling was achieved by sponging a second color over the first, and then spattering spray paint over the whole part—short spurts work best. Attach the Roof and Legs with glue. Glue the painted dowel into the perch hole.

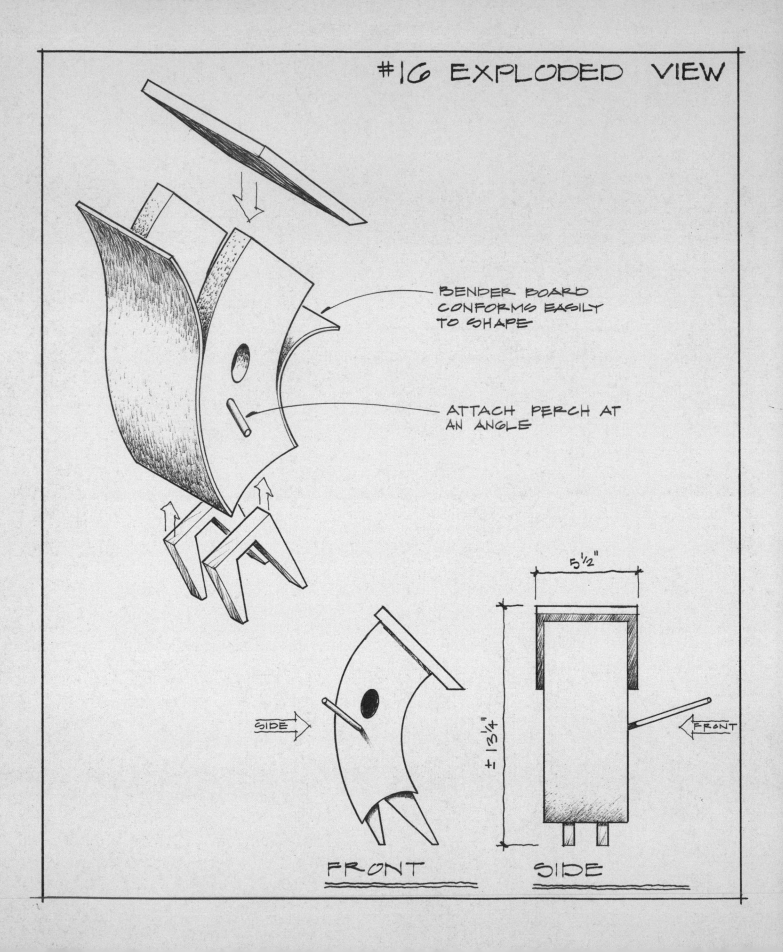

16 EXPLODED VIEW

BENDER BOARD CONFORMS EASILY TO SHAPE

ATTACH PERCH AT AN ANGLE

SIDE →

FRONT

← FRONT

5½"

± 13¼"

SIDE

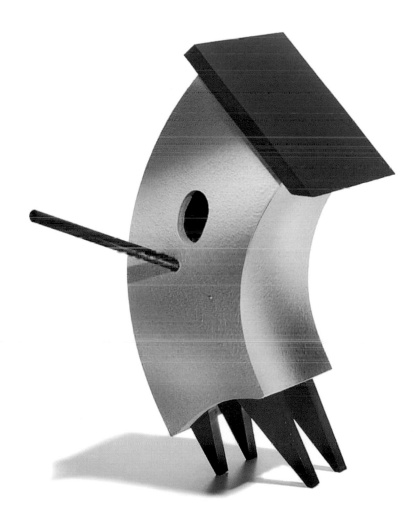

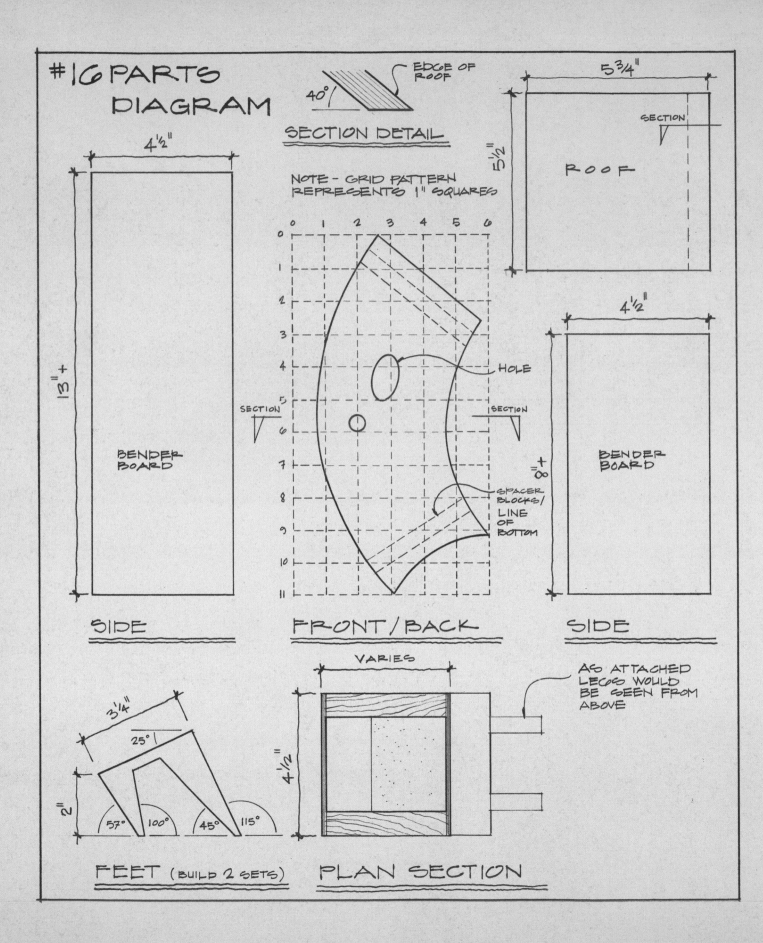

#16 PARTS DIAGRAM

SECTION DETAIL

40° EDGE OF ROOF

NOTE - GRID PATTERN REPRESENTS 1" SQUARES

5¾"
5½"
ROOF

4½"
13"+
BENDER BOARD
SIDE

0 1 2 3 4 5 6
0 1 2 3 4 5 6 7 8 9 10 11

HOLE
SECTION
SECTION
SPACER BLOCKS / LINE OF BOTTOM

FRONT/BACK

4½"
8"+
BENDER BOARD
SIDE

3¼"
25°
2"
57° 100° 45° 115°

FEET (BUILD 2 SETS)

VARIES
4½"

AS ATTACHED LEGOS WOULD BE SEEN FROM ABOVE

PLAN SECTION

16 TOOLS

Damp rag for glue drips
Drill
Drill bit for entrance and perch
Hammer, screwdriver, or stapler
Sander or sandpaper
Saw

SUPPLIES

Bender board
Latex paint
MDF or plywood
Nails, screws, or wood staples
Spray paint
Wood putty or spackle
½" wooden dowel
Yellow wood glue

INSTRUCTIONS ———————————

• Saw the Front and Back pieces from the sheet material. A jigsaw or band saw works best. If you would like the entrance hole to be oval shaped, predrill a hole and then saw it to shape. Drill the perch hole at an angle.

• Saw the Sides out of bender board. Bender board is a type of thin plywood that is manufactured to bend around curves. To find it, try a lumber store or look in the business section of the telephone directory under plywood. Saw the spacer blocks from sheet material. Begin assembling the birdhouse by attaching the top and bottom blocks, which are shown as dotted lines on the Parts Diagram, to the Front and Back before attaching the Sides. These blocks permanently stay in the birdhouse. For each Side, start at one end wrap bender board around the edges of Front and Back pieces, applying glue and fasteners as you go. Once this is done, trim the excess off the other end.

• Fill any gaps or edge grain that shows around the front edge with wood putty. Sand these areas smooth. An electric sander will work best here, but, with a bit more elbow grease, sandpaper wrapped around a wood block will also work.

• Saw the Roof and the Feet from plywood or MDF. A jigsaw or band saw will work best for cutting out the Feet. You may want to temporarily assemble the parts with hot glue or masking tape to see how the birdhouse balances, in case you need to adjust the Feet placement or length.

• I painted all of the parts before I assembled them so that I didn't have to mask anything. Paint all parts with two or more coats of latex paint, sanding lightly between coats. The fade effect on the Feet was accomplished with spray paint. Paint the main base color and then once that is dry, spray the tips. Temporarily glue them to a scrap board to hold them while you paint them and until they dry.

• Attach the Roof and Feet with glue. Glue the painted dowel into the perch hole.

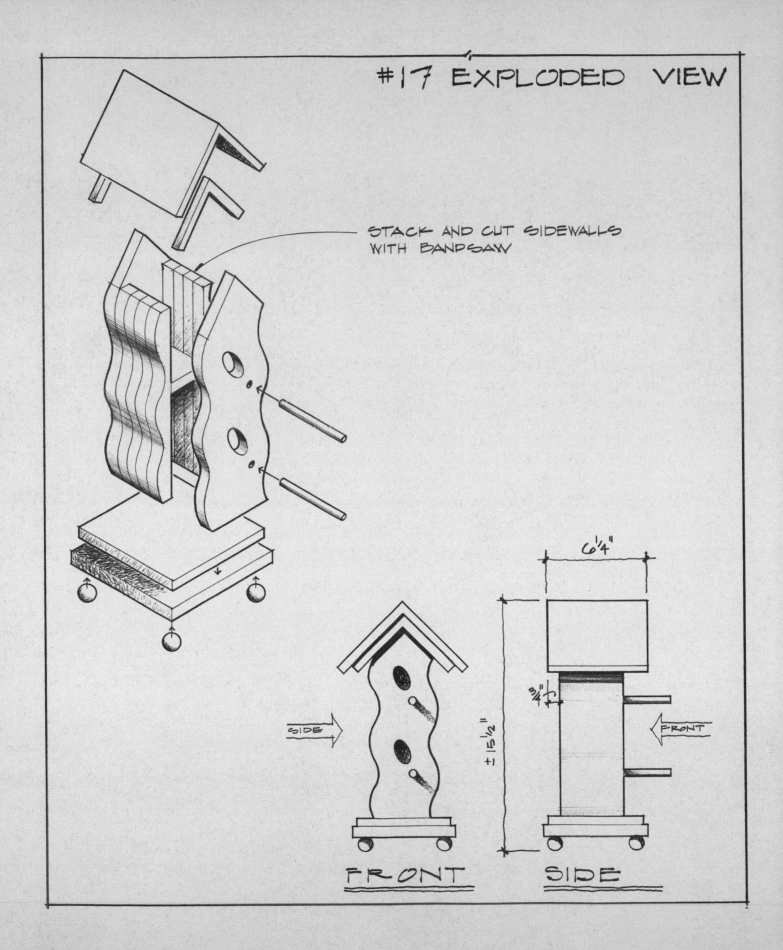

#17 EXPLODED VIEW

STACK AND CUT SIDEWALLS
WITH BANDSAW

SIDE →

← FRONT

6 1/4"

3/4"

± 15 1/2"

FRONT   SIDE

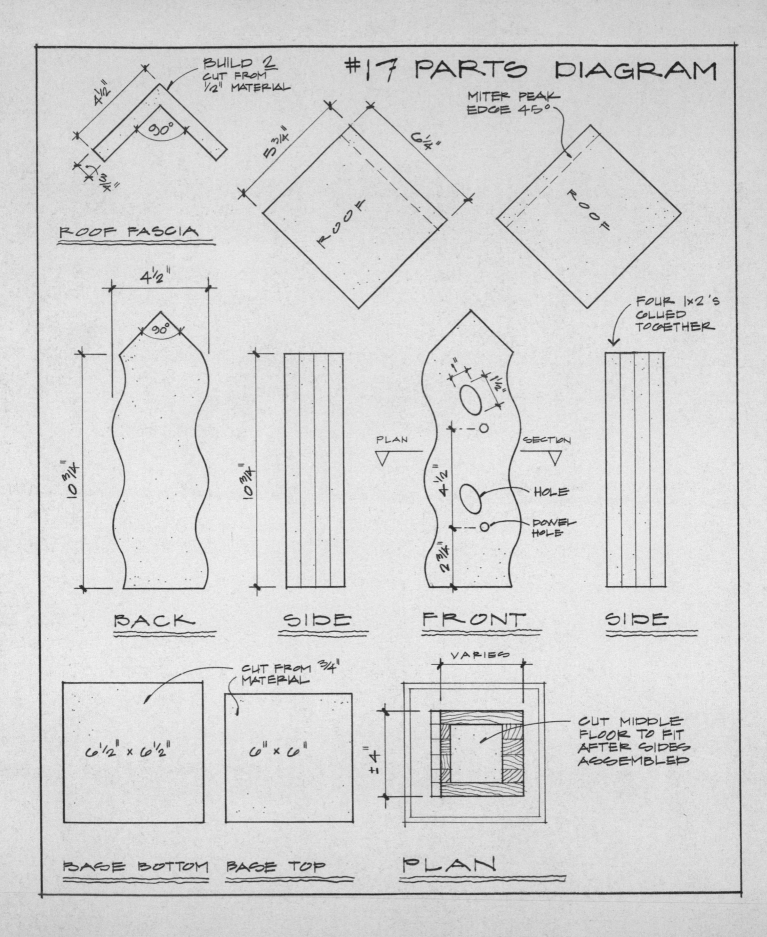

#17 PARTS DIAGRAM

BUILD 2
CUT FROM
1/2" MATERIAL

4 1/2"

3/4"

90°

ROOF FASCIA

5 3/4"

6 1/4"

ROOF

MITER PEAK
EDGE 45°

ROOF

FOUR 1x2's
GLUED
TOGETHER

4 1/2"

90°

10 3/4"

10 3/4"

PLAN

SECTION

1"

1 1/2"

4 1/2"

2 3/4"

HOLE

DOWEL
HOLE

BACK

SIDE

FRONT

SIDE

CUT FROM 3/4"
MATERIAL

6 1/2" x 6 1/2"

6" x 6"

BASE BOTTOM

BASE TOP

VARIES

+4"

CUT MIDDLE
FLOOR TO FIT
AFTER SIDES
ASSEMBLED

PLAN

17 TOOLS

Damp rag for glue drips
Drill
Drill bit for entrance and perch
Hammer, screwdriver, or stapler
Sander or sandpaper
Saw

SUPPLIES

Latex paint
MDF, pine boards, or plywood
Nails, screws, or wood staples
Spray paint
Wood putty or spackle
Wooden beads (4)
½" wooden dowel
Yellow wood glue

INSTRUCTIONS

• Saw the Front and Back pieces from the sheet material. Saw the Sides out of stacked layers of MDF or pine boards. A jigsaw or band saw works best. If you have a band saw, you can glue the stack of Side pieces and then cut the curves. If not, assemble the Side pieces by stacking and gluing between each layer. Small nails can also be used to hold the layers together. Take care not to split the wood. If you are using MDF, it can be very difficult to nail, as it is very dense. You may find it easier if you first drill a pilot hole for each nail.

• If you would like the entrance holes to be oval shaped, predrill a hole and then cut them to shape. Drill the perch holes now before the parts are assembled.

• Fill any gaps or edge grain that shows on the sides with wood putty. Sand these areas smooth. An electric drum sander will work best here, but, with a bit more elbow grease, sandpaper wrapped around a wood dowel will also work to smooth the curved surfaces. Saw the Roof and the Base pieces from plywood or MDF.

• I painted all of the parts before I assembled them so that I didn't have to mask anything. Paint all parts with two or more coats of latex paint, sanding lightly between coats. The fade effect on the main body of the birdhouse was accomplished with spray paint over a different color of latex. Paint the main base color and then once that is dry, spray from one end to achieve the fade. The Base was coated in black paint and then spattered with flat white. To do this, hold the spray paint nozzle about two feet from the part and use short, quick spurts. Experiment on a scrap piece first. Once you start to paint the birdhouse, if you don't like it, you can always start over and paint it again. The wooden beads for the feet are sprayed gloss black.

• Attach the Roof and Base with glue. Attach the feet to the Base with screws through the holes of the beads. Glue the painted dowels into the perch holes. You may need to sand the end of the dowels to fit.

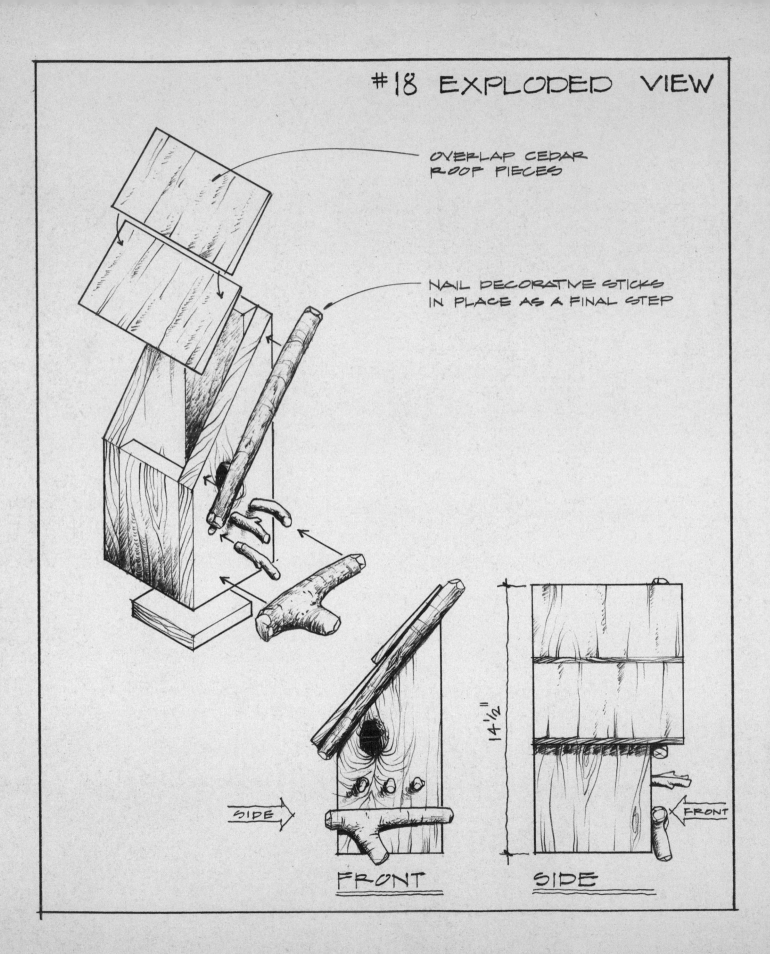

#18 EXPLODED VIEW

OVERLAP CEDAR
ROOF PIECES

NAIL DECORATIVE STICKS
IN PLACE AS A FINAL STEP

14 1/2"

SIDE →

FRONT

← FRONT

SIDE

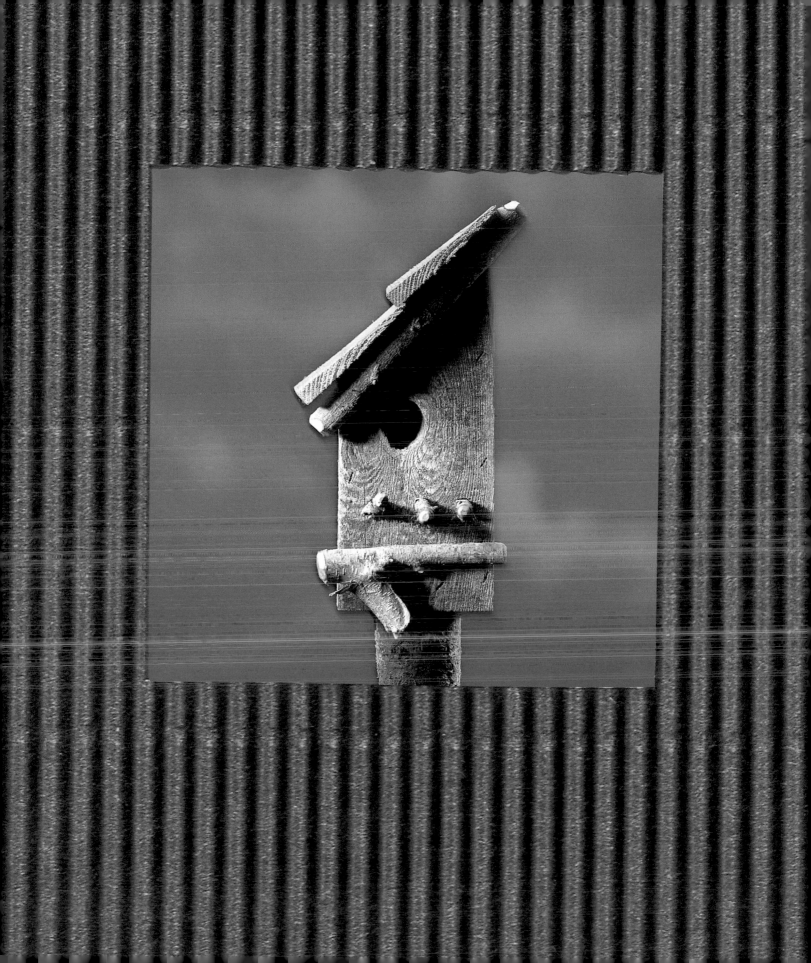

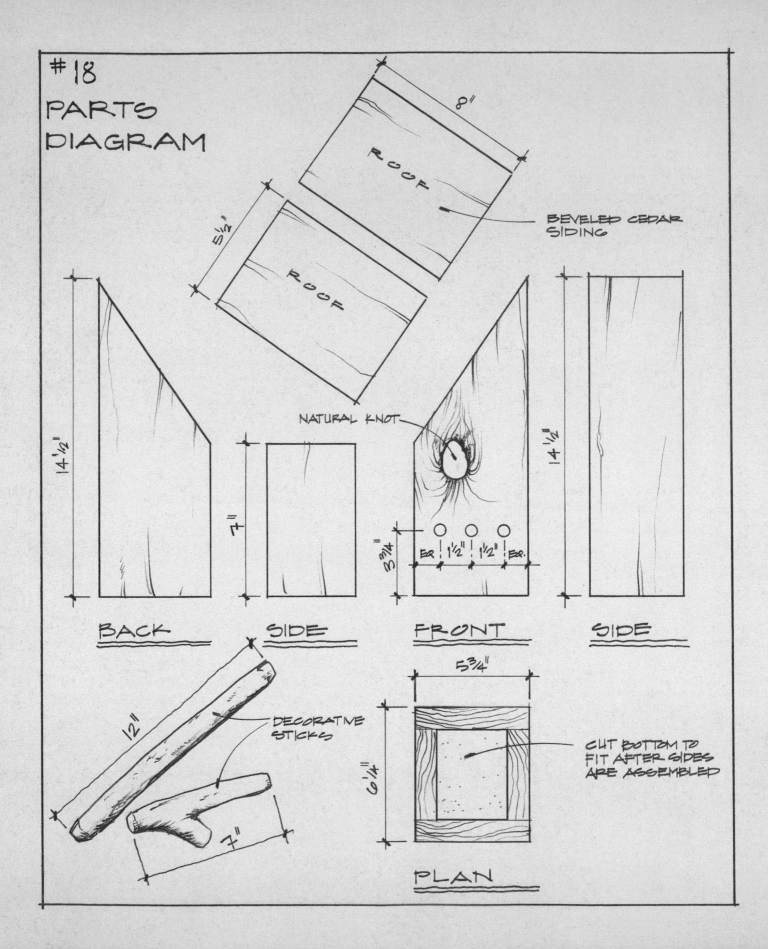

#18
PARTS
DIAGRAM

8"

ROOF

5½"

ROOF

BEVELED CEDAR
SIDING

14½"

NATURAL KNOT

14½"

7"

5¾"

EQ. 1½" 1½" EQ.

BACK   SIDE   FRONT   SIDE

12"

DECORATIVE
STICKS

7"

5¾"

6¼"

CUT BOTTOM TO
FIT AFTER SIDES
ARE ASSEMBLED

PLAN

18   TOOLS

Damp rag for glue drips
Drill
Drill bit for entrance and perches
Hammer, screwdriver, or stapler
Saw

SUPPLIES

Assorted decorative sticks
Cedar siding
Nails, screws, or wood staples
Rough wood boards
Yellow wood glue

INSTRUCTIONS

• Saw the flat pieces from the wood boards. If you can, choose a board with natural knot holes for the entrance. If not, then drill the entrance hole on the Front now, or wait until the birdhouse is built and drill it last.

• I find it easier to assemble the four sides first, overlapping the Back first to the two Side pieces. Apply glue to each joint as you assemble it. Keep a damp rag handy to wipe up glue drips while they are wet.

• If the sides don't go together square (which is common with old wood), take this opportunity to straighten the four corners by gently pushing or hammering it square while the glue is still wet. Once the four sides are together, insert the Bottom. If you want the Bottom removable for cleaning, use screws and no glue to attach it. Saw the Bottom slightly smaller to help it go in easier. The cracks that are left where it meets the sides allow for drainage once you put it to use outside. For additional drainage, you may want to drill a couple of ¼" holes in the base.

• The Roof is two pieces of beveled cedar siding overlapped. Attach the Roof with glue and fasteners. The Back can be flush if you intend to wall mount this birdhouse. Drill a small hole on the Back near the top to hang it on a nail.

• The perches are made up of decorative sticks. Hold them up to your structure to decide where they look best. If left a little long, they can add character. If you like, sand these pieces at each end with sandpaper or a sander to slightly round them. Drill holes for the perches. If needed, sand the end that goes in the birdhouse to fit. Apply a bit of glue before pushing them in. You may also want to hammer a small nail in at an angle through the perch into the Front of the birdhouse. If you do this, it's less obvious if done from the bottom. Drill a pilot hole first to prevent splitting the perch. A birdhouse built out of these natural materials will quickly age to a nice grey.

The decorative sticks you choose can provide personality for your creation. I try to collect many more of these pieces than I think I'll need so that I am not limited in my possibilities. Keep your eyes open year-round.

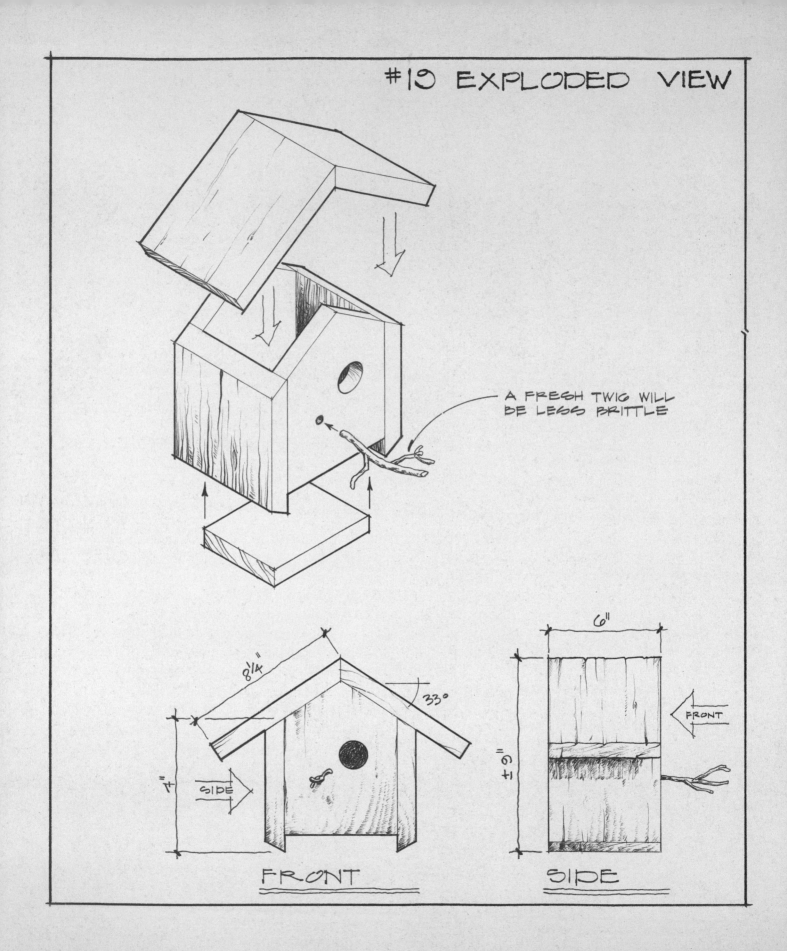

#19 EXPLODED VIEW

A FRESH TWIG WILL
BE LESS BRITTLE

8¼"

33°

7"

SIDE

FRONT

6"

FRONT

9¼"

SIDE

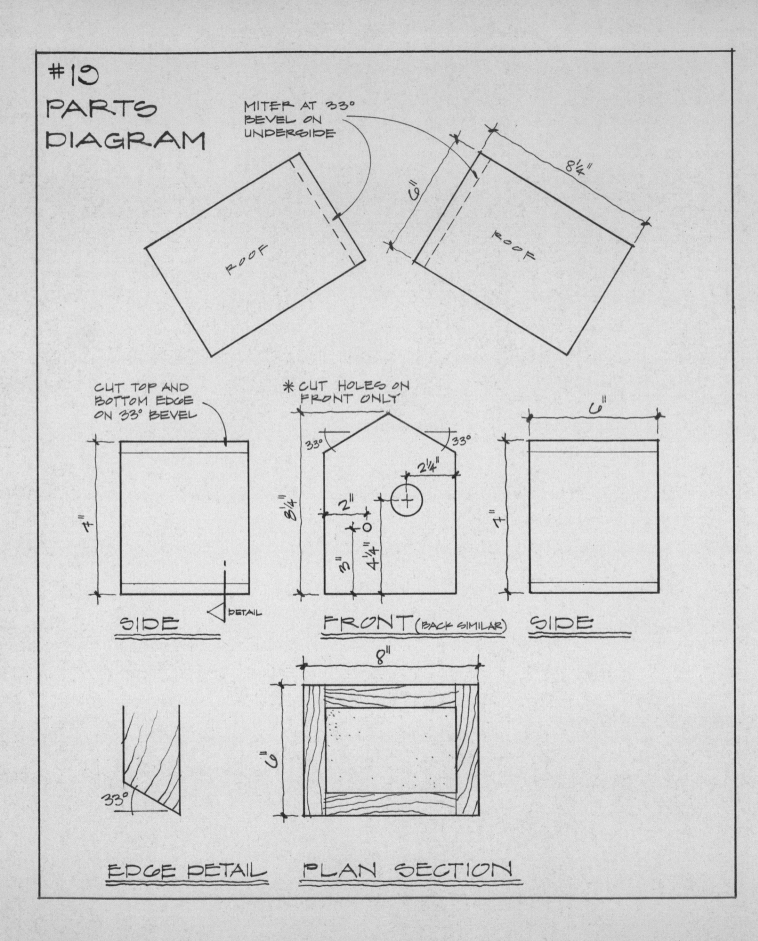

#19
PARTS
DIAGRAM

MITER AT 33°
BEVEL ON
UNDERSIDE

ROOF

ROOF

8¼"

6"

CUT TOP AND
BOTTOM EDGE
ON 33° BEVEL

* CUT HOLES ON
FRONT ONLY

7"

33°   33°

8¼"

2¼"

2"

6"

7"

3"   4¼"

DETAIL

SIDE   FRONT (BACK SIMILAR)   SIDE

8"

6"

33°

EDGE DETAIL   PLAN SECTION

19 TOOLS

Damp rag for glue drips
Drill
Drill bit for entrance and perches
Hammer, screwdriver, or stapler
Saw

SUPPLIES

Nails, screws, or wood staples
Rough wood boards
Twig
Yellow wood glue

INSTRUCTIONS ————————

- Saw the flat pieces from the wood boards. If you can, choose a board with a natural knot hole for the entrance. If not, then drill the entrance hole now on the Front, or wait until it is built and drill it last.

- I find it easier to assemble the four sides first, overlapping the Side pieces to the Back and Front pieces. Apply yellow glue to each joint as you assemble it. Keep a damp rag handy to wipe up glue drips while they are wet.

- If the sides don't go together square (which is common with old wood), take this opportunity to straighten the four corners by gently pushing or hammering it square while the glue is still wet. Once the four sides are together, insert the Bottom. If you want the Bottom removable for cleaning, use screws and no glue to attach it. Saw the Bottom slightly smaller to help it go in easier. The cracks that are left where it meets the sides allow for drainage once you put it to use outside. For additional drainage, you may want to drill a couple of ¼" holes in the Bottom.

- The Roof is two pieces beveled at the peak. Attach the Roof with glue and fasteners. The Back can be flush if you intend to wall mount this birdhouse. Drill a small hole on the Back near the top to hang it on a nail.

- The twig you choose for the perch can provide personality for your creation. Hold it up to your structure to decide where it looks best. If placed off center, it can add character. Drill a hole about the diameter of the perch. If needed, sand the end that goes in the birdhouse to fit. Apply a bit of glue before pushing it in. You may also want to hammer a small nail in at an angle through the perch into the Front of the birdhouse. If you do this, it's less obvious if done from the bottom. Drill a tiny pilot hole first to prevent splitting the perch.

- The boards that I chose for this birdhouse had a wonderful weathered grey surface. Even if you choose new raw cedar, a birdhouse built out of natural materials will quickly age to a nice grey. After one season outside, it will look like it has been around for decades.

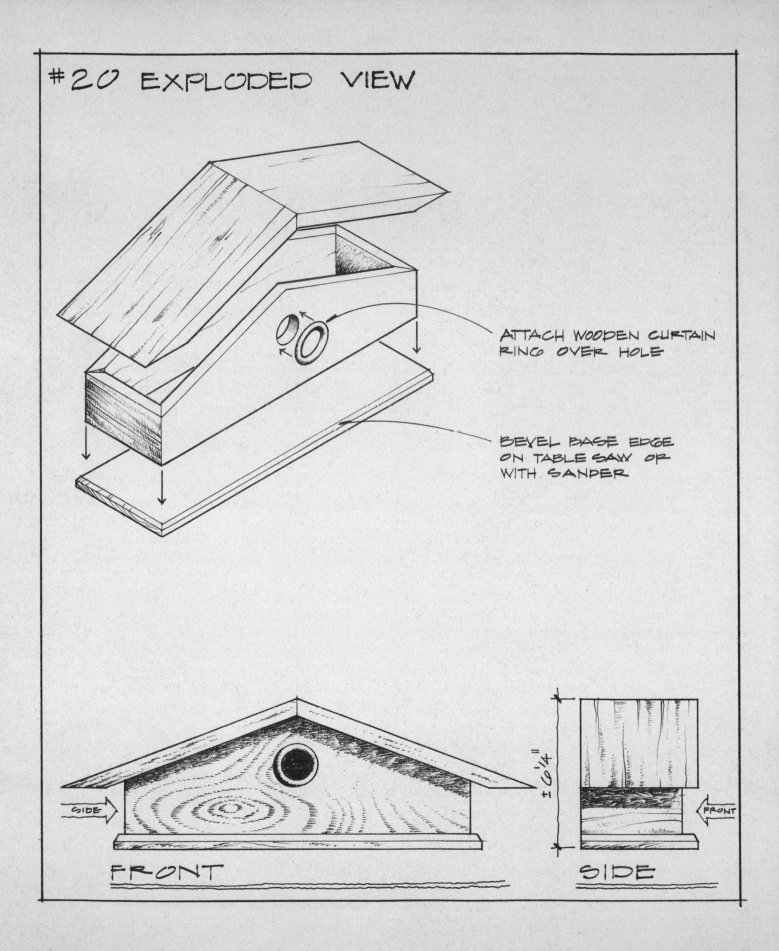

#20 EXPLODED VIEW

ATTACH WOODEN CURTAIN RING OVER HOLE

BEVEL BASE EDGE ON TABLE SAW OR WITH SANDER

SIDE

FRONT

FRONT

$\pm 6\frac{1}{4}''$

FRONT

SIDE

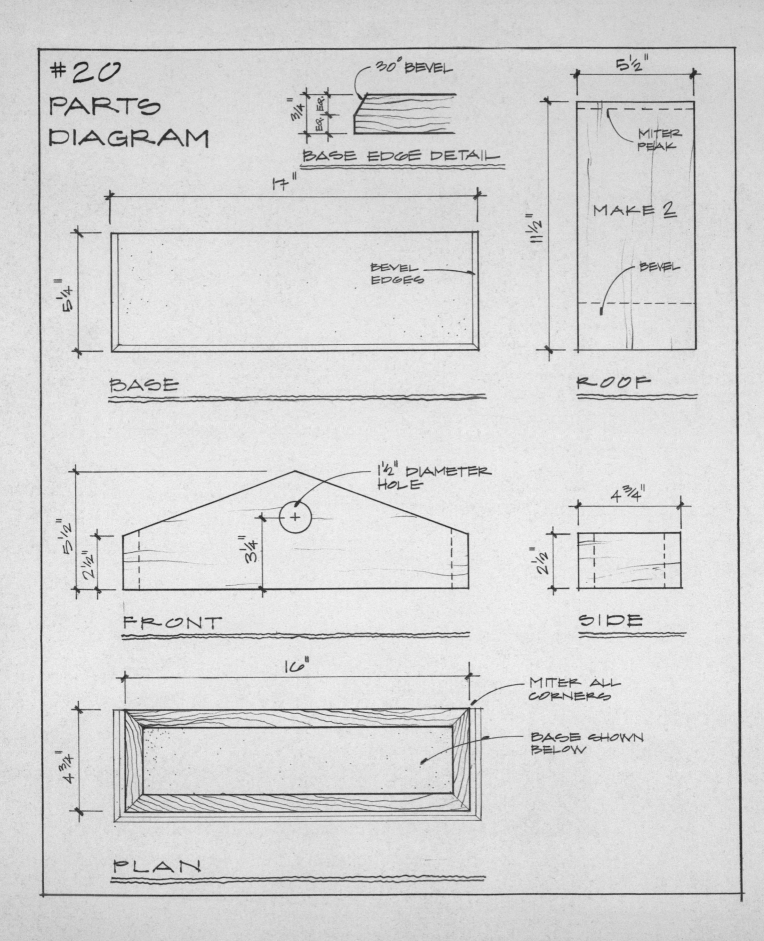

#20 PARTS DIAGRAM

30° BEVEL

BASE EDGE DETAIL

17"

5¼"

BEVEL EDGES

BASE

5½"

MITER PEAK

MAKE 2

BEVEL

ROOF

1½" DIAMETER HOLE

5½"

2½"

3¼"

FRONT

4¾"

2½"

SIDE

16"

MITER ALL CORNERS

BASE SHOWN BELOW

4¾"

PLAN

20 TOOLS

Damp rag for glue drips
Drill
Drill bit for entrance hole
Hammer, screwdriver, or stapler
Saw

SUPPLIES

Black latex paint
Clear acrylic spray paint
Colored pencils or markers
Latex paint
Nails, screws, or wood staples
Wood boards
Wood putty or spackle
Wooden curtain ring
Yellow wood glue

INSTRUCTIONS ————————

• Saw the flat pieces from the wood boards. Miter the ends as indicated. Assemble the four sides. Use finishing nails (a nail with little or no head) if you don't want the nail holes to be obvious. Apply glue to each joint as you assemble it. Keep a damp rag handy to wipe up glue drips while they are wet. Place the Base on the bottom of the birdhouse and nail or screw it in place. Don't use glue if you want the Base removable.

• Attach the Roof pieces. The Roof should sit flush with the Back. Drill a hole in the Back near the top if you wish to hang it.

• Drill the entrance hole slightly smaller than the inside diameter of the wooden curtain ring. Glue the ring in place. If it is going to be placed outdoors, secure the ring with nails. If you use finishing nails, it is best to drill a small pilot hole through the ring first so you don't split it. If desired, this would be a good time to fill the nail holes with wood putty. Sand lightly if needed, but don't sand the woodgrain smooth.

• Although the paint technique on this particular birdhouse is relatively simple, it may require some practice. Paint the whole structure with black latex paint. Then, using lighter colors of latex, apply the color to the surface. If you use strokes across the grain it will help accentuate it. Remember, if you don't like it you can always start over and paint it again. Work with different colors to see what different effects you can achieve. This part takes some time, but your patience will pay off.

• Once this birdhouse was painted and dry, I used colored pencils and markers to draw a woodgrain effect on the surface. Apply a clear acrylic spray paint to preserve the finish. Decorate the birdhouse with a fun creature, if you wish. The grasshopper that I chose catches viewers off guard as it is way out of scale.

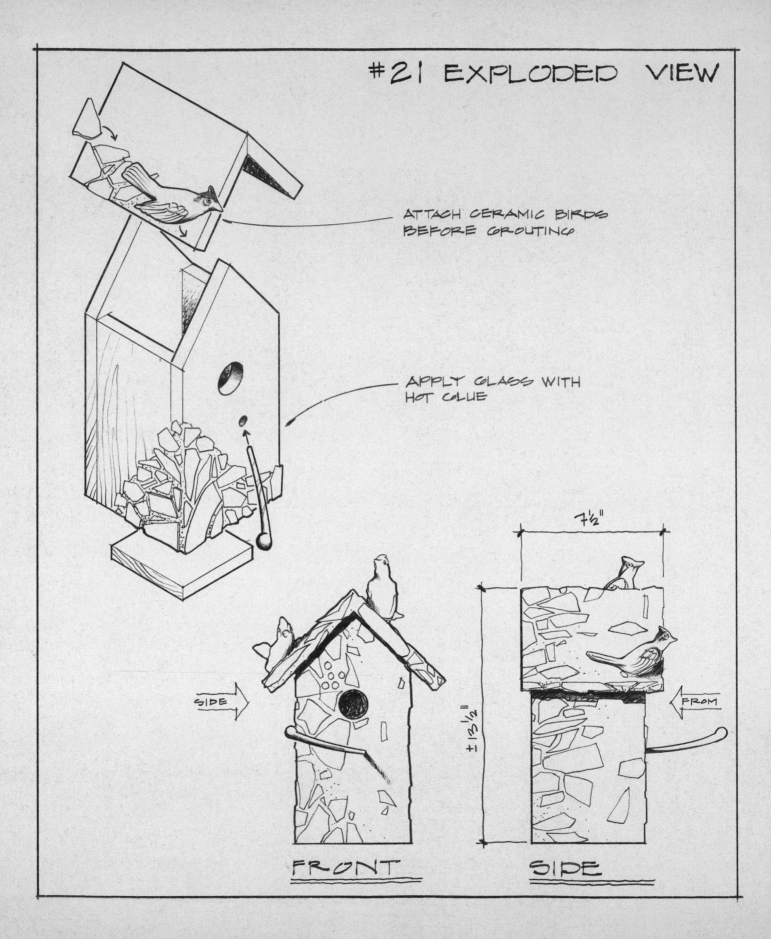

#21 EXPLODED VIEW

ATTACH CERAMIC BIRDS
BEFORE GROUTING

APPLY GLASS WITH
HOT GLUE

7½"

± 13½"

SIDE

FROM

FRONT

SIDE

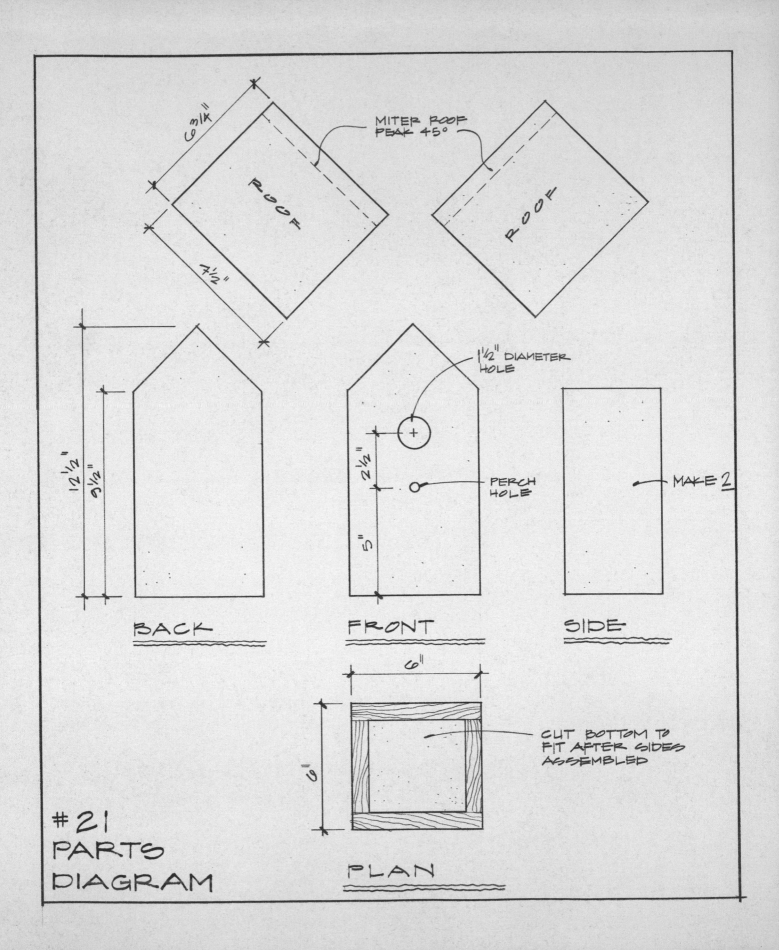

MITER ROOF
PEAK 45°

ROOF

6 3/4"

7 1/2"

ROOF

BACK

12 1/2"

9 1/2"

FRONT

1 1/2" DIAMETER HOLE

2 1/2"

PERCH HOLE

5"

SIDE

MAKE 2

21
PARTS
DIAGRAM

PLAN

6"

6"

CUT BOTTOM TO FIT AFTER SIDES ASSEMBLED

21

TOOLS

Drill
Drill bits for entrance and perch
Goggles
Hammer, screwdriver, or stapler
Hot-glue gun and glue sticks
Saw
Soft cloth or diaper
Work gloves

SUPPLIES

Broken art glass pieces
Ceramic figurines
Nails, screws, or wood staples
½" or ¾" OSB or plywood
Tile grout
Yellow wood glue

INSTRUCTIONS ———————

• Saw the flat pieces from the sheet material. Measure and drill the entrance and perch holes now while the Front piece can be held flat. Assemble the four sides, the Base, and the Roof, using fasteners and glue.

• Collect enough art glass pieces to more than cover all surfaces of the birdhouse. You will be amazed at how much it will take, and you'll want a good assortment to choose from. Find a glass blowing studio in your community and see if they will sell or give you broken or unusable pieces. Flat pieces, such as plates, work best. Wearing goggles and work gloves, wrap the glass in a cloth and break it into workable pieces by hitting it with the hammer. This part can be fun and stress relieving. If you can get the glass studio to re-fire the glass pieces to round over the edges, they will be much safer to handle.

• The perch I chose is a glass rod left over from some other glass creation. Antique or second hand stores are a wonderful source for ceramic figurines. The two ceramic birds perched on the roof of this birdhouse house previously sat together on an antique vase. Wearing goggles, I used a hammer and screwdriver to gently tap where they joined and break them apart. This can be difficult to predict where to tap, so have a second choice available if you shatter your first. If they break into larger pieces, you may be able to glue them back together.

• Lay the birdhouse on its side so that you are working on a horizontal surface. Apply hot glue to the back of each clean, dry piece of art glass. Take care not to burn or cut yourself. Attach the birds and perch as you work. Try to leave about an ⅛" gap between the mosaic of glass. The glass must be securely attached or you will have trouble with the next step.

• Apply tile grout, following manufacturer's instructions. The grout is available in many colors from home improvement stores. Mix it to about the consistency of cake frosting and work it between the glass. Keep working with it as it dries by rubbing off any excess with a soft cloth. This part should be done wearing gloves. The edges of broken glass are very sharp. Again, take care not to cut yourself. Keep rinsing and wringing out your cloth as you go. This part seems to go on forever. Finish with a clean dry cloth. Buff until the glass is clean.

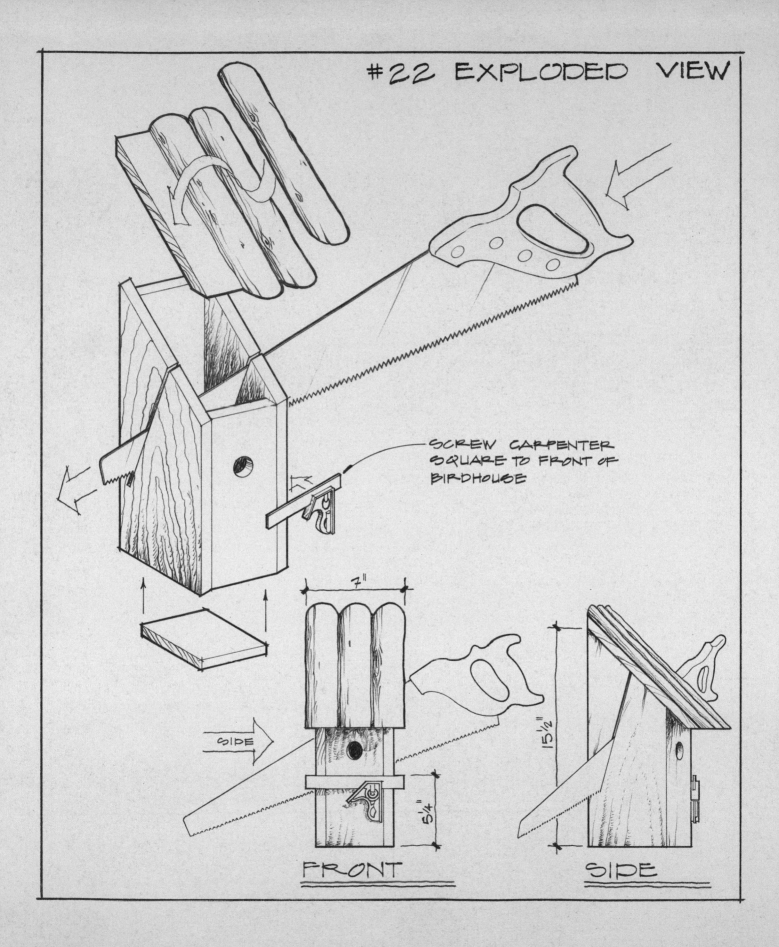

#22 EXPLODED VIEW

SCREW CARPENTER SQUARE TO FRONT OF BIRDHOUSE

SIDE

7"

15½"

5¼"

FRONT

SIDE

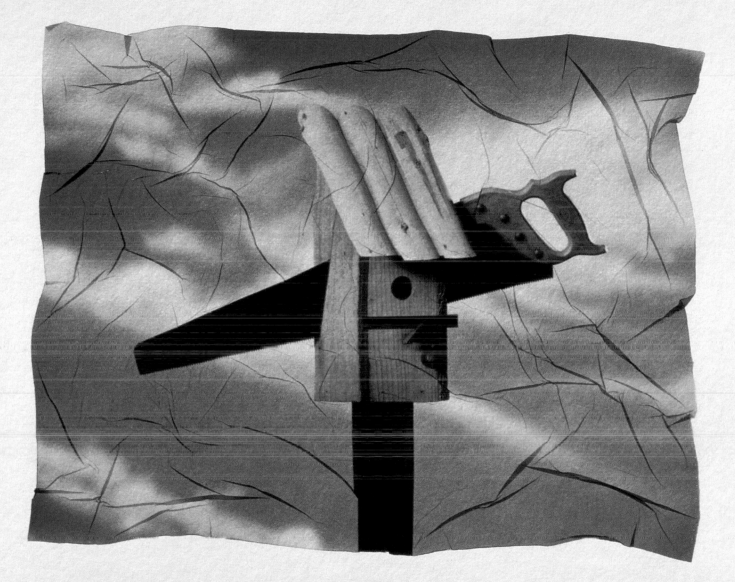

This Old Birdhouse

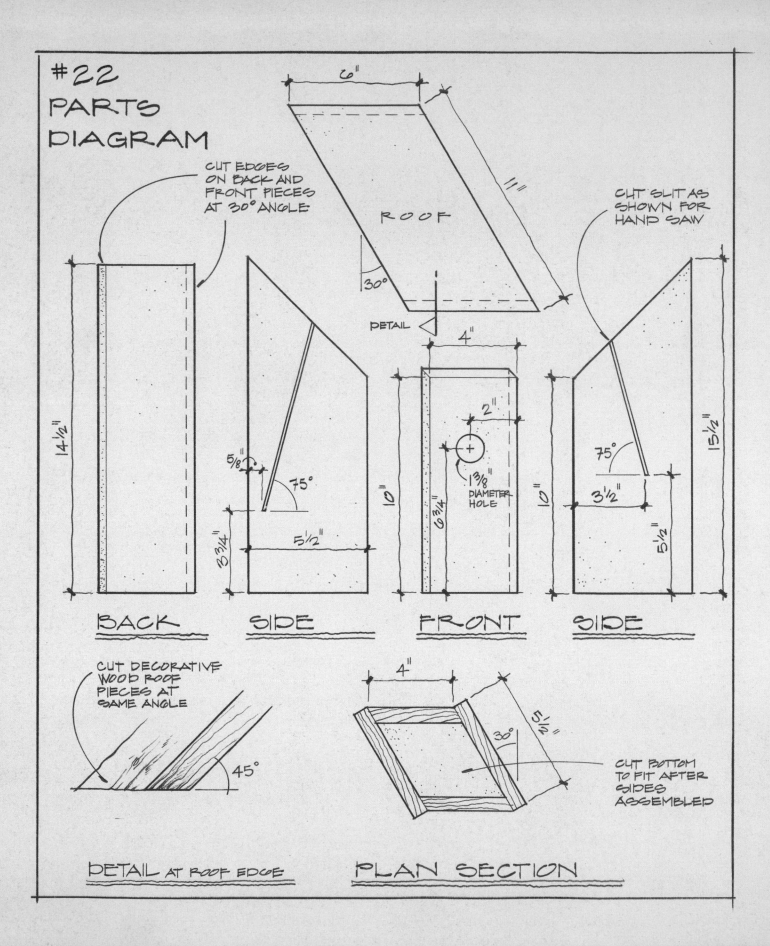

#22 PARTS DIAGRAM

CUT EDGES ON BACK AND FRONT PIECES AT 30° ANGLE

CUT SLIT AS SHOWN FOR HAND SAW

6"

ROOF

11"

30°

DETAIL

14½"

5/8"

75°

3¾"

5½"

BACK

SIDE

4"

2"

1⅜" DIAMETER HOLE

10"

9¾"

FRONT

75°

3½"

5½"

10"

15½"

SIDE

CUT DECORATIVE WOOD ROOF PIECES AT SAME ANGLE

45°

DETAIL AT ROOF EDGE

4"

30°

5½"

CUT BOTTOM TO FIT AFTER SIDES ASSEMBLED

PLAN SECTION

22 TOOLS

Damp rag for glue drips
Drill
Drill bit for entrance hole
Hammer, screwdriver, or stapler
Pencil
Saw

SUPPLIES

Carpenter's square
Nails, screws, or wood staples
Old hand saw
Peeled log
Rough wood boards
Yellow wood glue

INSTRUCTIONS ——————

• Saw the flat pieces from the wood boards. If you can, choose a board with a natural knot hole for the entrance. If the knot is still in place but loose, knock it out with the hammer and a screwdriver. If not, drill the entrance hole on the Front now, or wait until it is built and drill it last.

• Assemble the four sides first. On this particular birdhouse I overlapped the Side pieces over the Front and Back pieces, insetting the Front slightly. Apply glue to each joint as you assemble it. Keep a damp rag handy to wipe up glue drips while they are wet. I like to start with the Back first because it gives you a chance to get used to how the wood reacts to the fasteners you've chosen.

• I purposely cut the Front and Back on a bevel so that the house would not be square. Once the four sides are together, insert the Bottom. If you want the Bottom removable for cleaning, use screws and no glue to attach it. For additional drainage, you may want to drill a couple of ¼" holes in the Bottom. Drill a small hole in the Back near the top if you are going to want to hang it.

• Decide where you want the saw to be placed and lightly draw a cut line with a pencil from the top of each sidewall down. Using the actual hand saw, carefully cut down into the birdhouse, using slow, deliberate strokes. You may also use a jig saw for this part, which will make it a bit easier and will give you a guide groove to cut with the hand saw. Once the hand saw is in place, leave it at the desired angle.

• Attach Roof. I used pieces of split, peeled log to cover the Roof piece. The piece will prevent rain from dripping through the cracks between the logs.

• Attach the carpenter's square with a couple of screws to the Front of the birdhouse. Placed outdoors, the metal elements will weather to create a rich, rust finish. This is a very good example of a unique birdhouse that can be decorated with recycled materials scavenged from your workshop or a local farm auction.

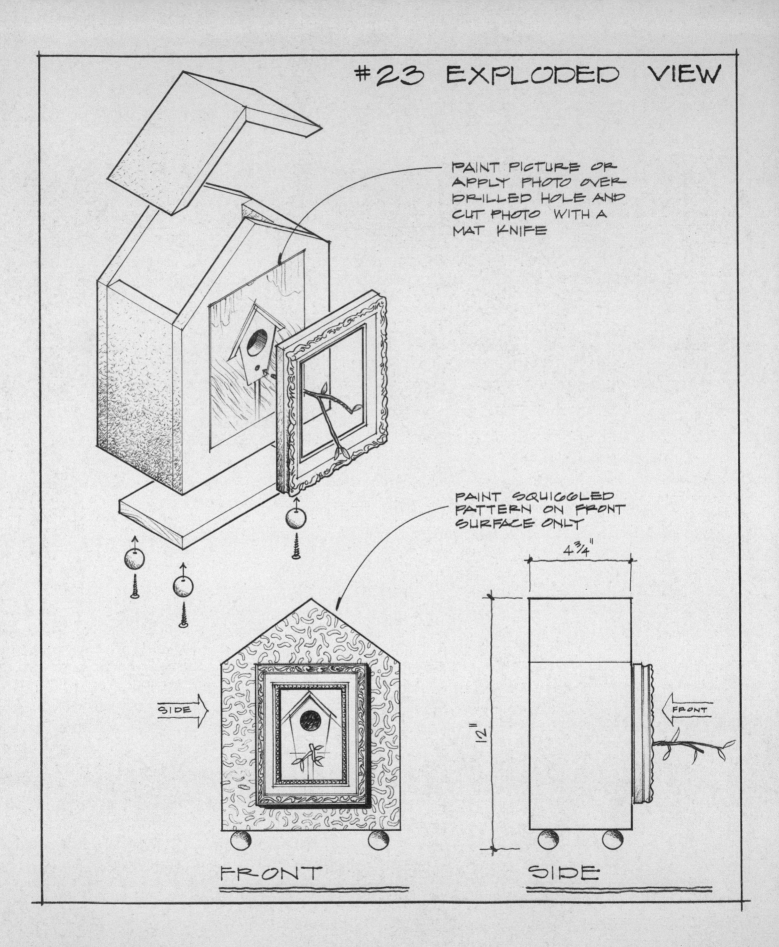

#23 EXPLODED VIEW

PAINT PICTURE OR APPLY PHOTO OVER DRILLED HOLE AND CUT PHOTO WITH A MAT KNIFE

PAINT SQUIGGLED PATTERN ON FRONT SURFACE ONLY

4 3/4"

SIDE

12"

FRONT

FRONT

FRONT

SIDE

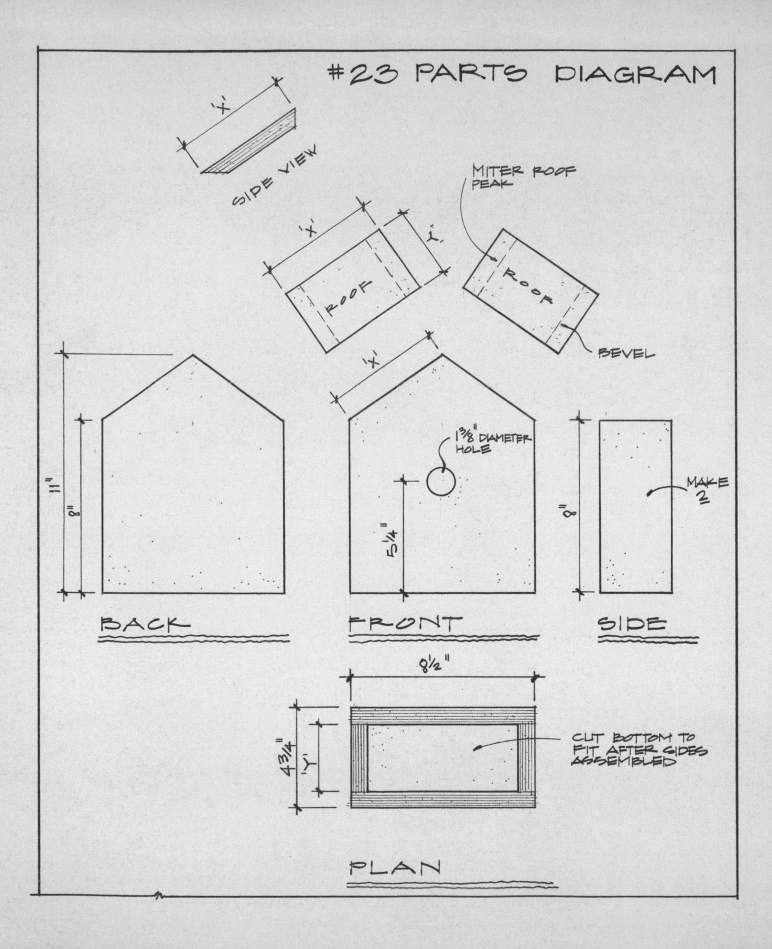

#23 PARTS DIAGRAM

SIDE VIEW

'X'

MITER ROOF PEAK

ROOF

'X'

'Y'

ROOF

BEVEL

BACK

11"

8"

FRONT

'X'

1 3/8" DIAMETER HOLE

5 1/4"

SIDE

8"

MAKE 2

PLAN

8 1/2"

4 3/4"

'Y'

CUT BOTTOM TO FIT AFTER SIDES ASSEMBLED

23 TOOLS

Damp rag for glue drips
Drill
Drill bit for entrance hole
Hammer, screwdriver, or stapler
Sandpaper
Saw
Small paintbrush

SUPPLIES

Flat black spray paint
Gloss black or clear paint
MDF or plywood
Nails, screws, or wood staples
Photo
Picture frame
Silk or paper leaves
Twig
Wood putty or spackle
Wooden beads (4)
Yellow wood glue

INSTRUCTIONS

• Saw the flat pieces from the sheet material. If you use MDF, you will have less trouble cleaning up the edges before you paint, as plywood leaves an exposed grain along the cut edge. Drill the entrance hole in the Front now, using a 1⅜" bit. Apply glue to each joint as you assemble the birdhouse. Keep a damp rag handy to wipe up glue drips while they are wet. Once the four sides are together, insert the Bottom. Fill the nail holes and any gaps and sand the whole birdhouse. Paint the wooden beads for the feet of the birdhouse. Attach the beads to the bottom with screws.

• The paint technique is relatively simple. Paint the entire birdhouse with flat black spray paint. The squiggles on the Front are gloss black paint applied with a small paintbrush. Clear gloss will yield the same effect. Practice on a scrap of painted wood first. The Roof and Side pieces were left flat black.

• Paint the miniature masterpiece directly on the Front surface of the birdhouse prior to attaching the frame. If you don't have the ability to paint the picture, glue a photo to the Front of the birdhouse and then cut out the hole. The picture frame was purchased at a store that sold framing supplies. Attach the frame with a minimal amount of glue. The inside edge of the frame will sit away from the Front enough to create some depth between it and the picture.

• The perch is a small twig with tiny leaves cut out of silk leaves or green paper and glued on. Insert the perch with a small dab of glue.

You can try something comical here if you like. Take a photo of a friend or relative with their mouth wide open and their hands up at their chest like they are holding a perch. Once developed, have the photo enlarged or copied so that their mouth is the proper size for the birdhouse entrance. Drill the perch hole where their hands are. If you don't tell them what the photo is for, imagine their surprise!

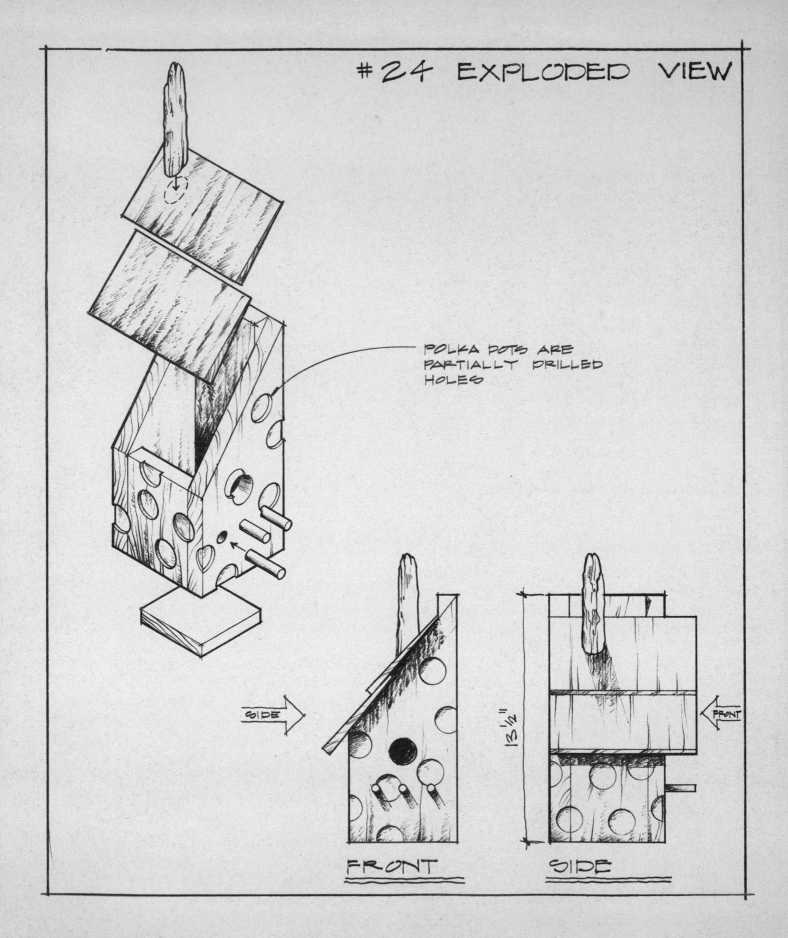

#24 EXPLODED VIEW

POLKA DOTS ARE
PARTIALLY DRILLED
HOLES

SIDE →

13½"

← FRONT

FRONT

SIDE

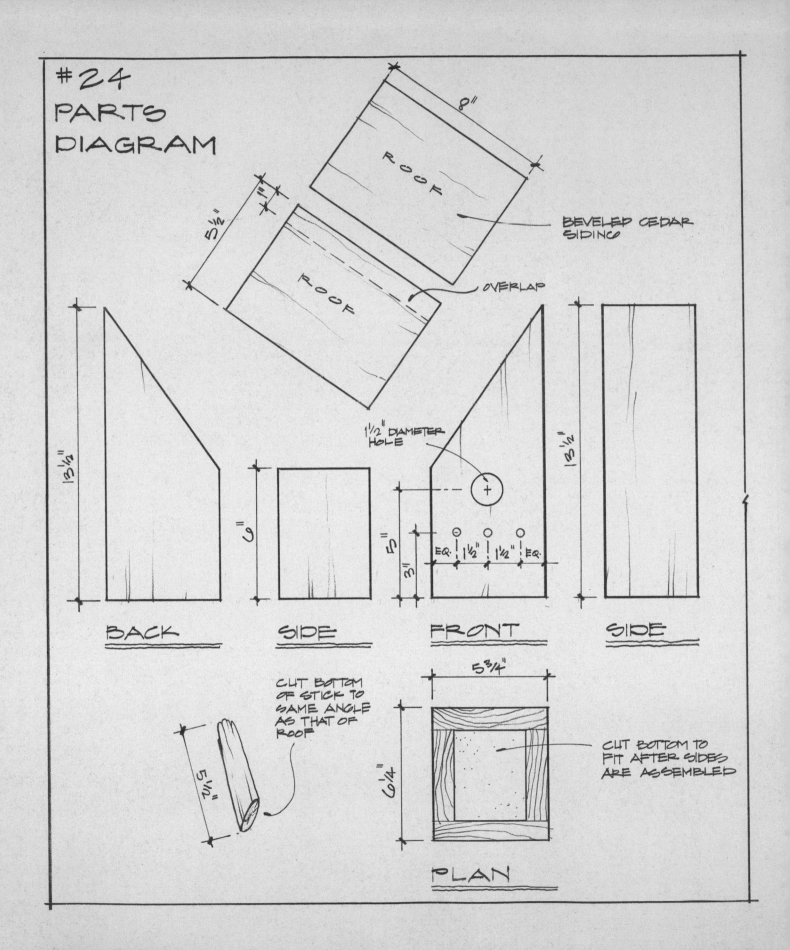

#24
PARTS
DIAGRAM

ROOF

8"

ROOF

5½"

1"

BEVELED CEDAR
SIDING

OVERLAP

BACK

13½"

SIDE

6"

FRONT

1½" DIAMETER
HOLE

5"

3"

EQ. | 1½" | 1½" | EQ.

SIDE

13½"

CUT BOTTOM
OF STICK TO
SAME ANGLE
AS THAT OF
ROOF

5½"

PLAN

5¾"

6¼"

CUT BOTTOM TO
FIT AFTER SIDES
ARE ASSEMBLED

24 TOOLS

Damp rag for glue drips
Drill
Drill bit for entrance and perches
Hammer or screwdriver
Saw

SUPPLIES

Assorted sticks
Cedar siding
Nails, screws, or wood staples
Rough wood boards
Yellow wood glue

INSTRUCTIONS ————————————

• Saw the flat pieces from the wood boards. If you can, choose a board with a natural knot hole for the entrance. If not, drill the entrance hole on the Front now, or wait until it is built and drill it last.

• I find it easier to assemble the four sides first, overlapping the Back first to the two Sides. Apply glue to each joint as you assemble it. Keep a damp rag handy to wipe up glue drips while they are wet.

• If the sides don't go together square (which is common with old wood), take this opportunity to straighten the four corners by gently pushing or hammering it square while the glue is still wet. Once the four sides are together, insert the Bottom. If you want the Bottom removable for cleaning, use screws and no glue to attach it. Saw the Bottom slightly smaller to help it go in easier. The cracks that are left where it meets the sides allow for drainage once you put it to use outside. For additional drainage, you may want to drill a couple of ¼" holes in the Bottom.

• The Roof is two pieces of beveled cedar siding overlapped. Attach the Roof with glue and fasteners. If you want to attach a large stick to the Roof to look like a smoke stack, cut the stick at the same angle and screw it onto the Roof from the underside prior to putting the Roof on the birdhouse. The back of the Roof can be flush if you intend to wall mount this birdhouse. Drill a small hole on the Back near the top to hang it on a nail.

• The polka dot pattern on this birdhouse was achieved with a paddle drill bit once the structure was assembled. With a hand drill or drill press, start on one side and drill holes about ¼" into the wood surface. These show up better in old, weathered, grey wood. Eventually these holes will weather too if not protected. Using a paddle bit will allow these spots to extend over the edge as long as the center of the drill bit is at least a ¼" from the edge and you go slow.

• Hold small sticks for the perches up to your structure to decide where they look best. Drill holes for these. If needed, sand the end that goes in the birdhouse to fit. Apply a bit of glue before pushing them in. You may also want to hammer a small nail in at an angle through the perches into the Front of the birdhouse. Drill pilot holes to prevent splitting the perches.

#25 PARTS DIAGRAM

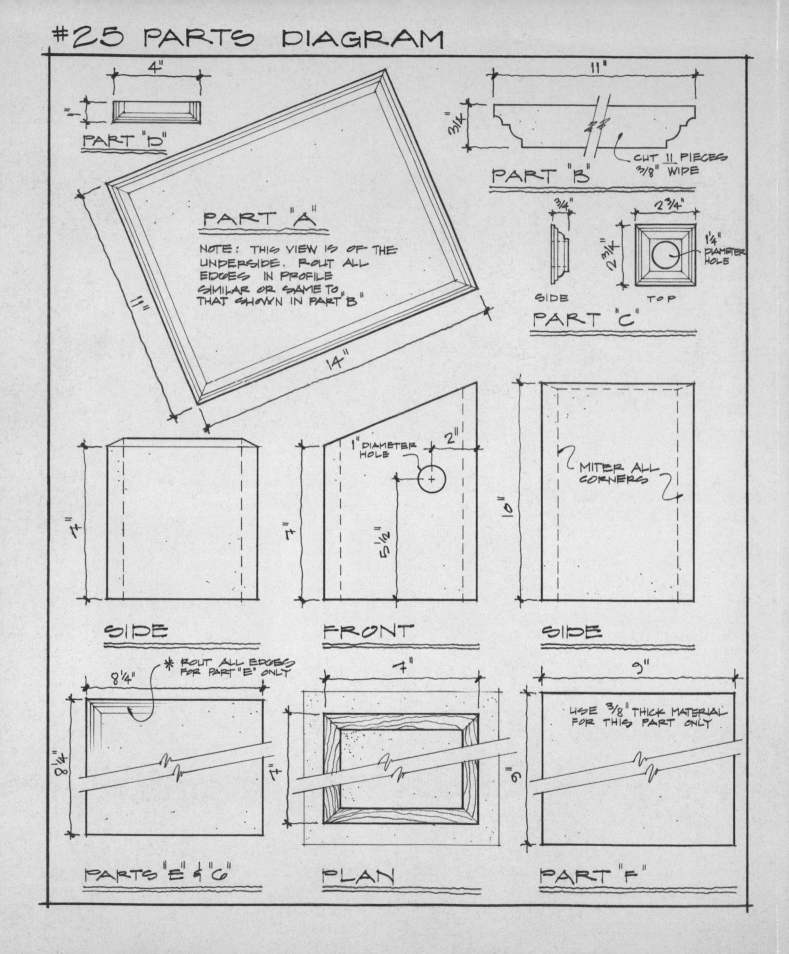

PART "D"
4"

PART "B"
11"
3/4"
CUT 11 PIECES 3/8" WIDE

PART "A"

NOTE: THIS VIEW IS OF THE UNDERSIDE. ROUT ALL EDGES IN PROFILE SIMILAR OR SAME TO THAT SHOWN IN PART "B"

11"
14"

PART "C"
3/4"
2 3/4"
2 3/4"
1 1/4" DIAMETER HOLE
SIDE
TOP

SIDE
7"

FRONT
1" DIAMETER HOLE
2"
7"
5 1/2"

SIDE
10"
MITER ALL CORNERS

PARTS "E" & "G"
* ROUT ALL EDGES FOR PART "E" ONLY
8 1/4"
8"

PLAN
7"
7"

PART "F"
9"
USE 3/8" THICK MATERIAL FOR THIS PART ONLY
6"

25 TOOLS

Cardboard and pins
Damp rag for glue drips
Drill
Drill bit for entrance hole
Hair dryer
Hammer or screwdriver
Router with bit
Saw
Waxed paper

SUPPLIES

Cedar shakes
MDF
Latex paint
Nails, screws or wood staples
Slow dry gold leaf sizing or crackle medium
Teacup
Twigs
Wood putty or spackle
Yellow wood glue and super glue

INSTRUCTIONS

• Saw the flat pieces from the MDF. Rout the Base and Roof pieces around the edge prior to assembly. Apply yellow glue to each joint as you assemble it. The piece around the front hole is a square of MDF that was routed while secured to the top of my workbench with a screw in the middle prior to drilling the hole. The hole in this decorative element was drilled slightly larger than the hole in the front wall of the birdhouse.

• To make the roof "rafters" I routed two opposite ends of a piece of MDF cut to the length of the rafters. This was then carefully split down into strips on a table saw. Extreme caution should be used when cutting thin strips. While the front three strips are left whole, the rest of the rafters are just the tips cut from the strips at the proper angle to match the wall. The decorative front square, rafters, and trellis base can be attached with yellow or hot glue.

• The miniature trellis was built prior to installation. Place a piece of waxed paper over a square of corrugated cardboard to use as a work surface. Pin it in the four corners. Wet the twigs for a few hours in hot water until they are pliable. Fresh twigs work best. Weave the twigs as desired and pin them to the cardboard to dry. When dry, apply a dab of super glue to the joints to hold them together. Cut the trellis to length.

• Paint the entire birdhouse with dark brown latex paint. After this dries, apply slow drying gold leaf sizing or crackle medium to all surfaces. These are readily available at home improvement, craft, or art supply stores. Apply the white latex paint while the sizing is still wet. The latex will want to bead up a bit, but that's OK. Now, blow over all surfaces with the hair dryer until it is dry The latex paint shrinks more than the sizing so it cracks. Apply more latex, if needed.

• Cut small shingles out of the rough cedar shakes and paint them with dark grey latex thinned with water. This will cause the latex to act like a stain. Attach the shingles to the birdhouse with glue and nails. Glue the trellis onto the birdhouse just before hanging the teacup. The teacup is hanging from an eye screw that was screwed into the eave of the house. Use a pair of pliers to open the eye screw, attach the teacup, and carefully close the eye screw again.

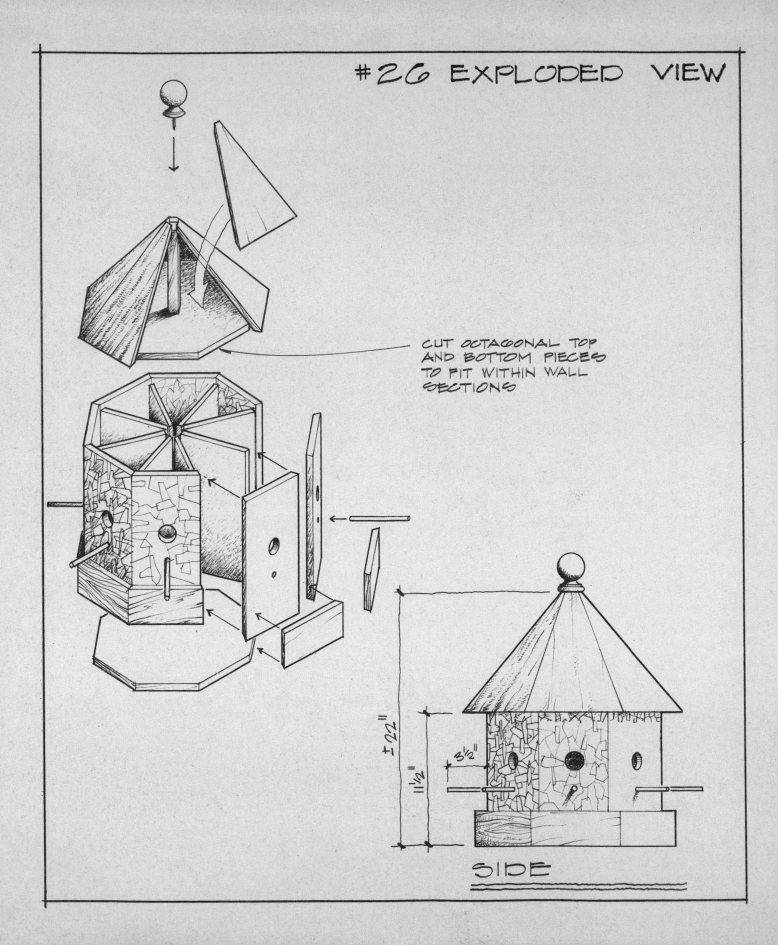

#26 EXPLODED VIEW

CUT OCTAGONAL TOP
AND BOTTOM PIECES
TO FIT WITHIN WALL
SECTIONS

± 22"

11½"

3½"

SIDE

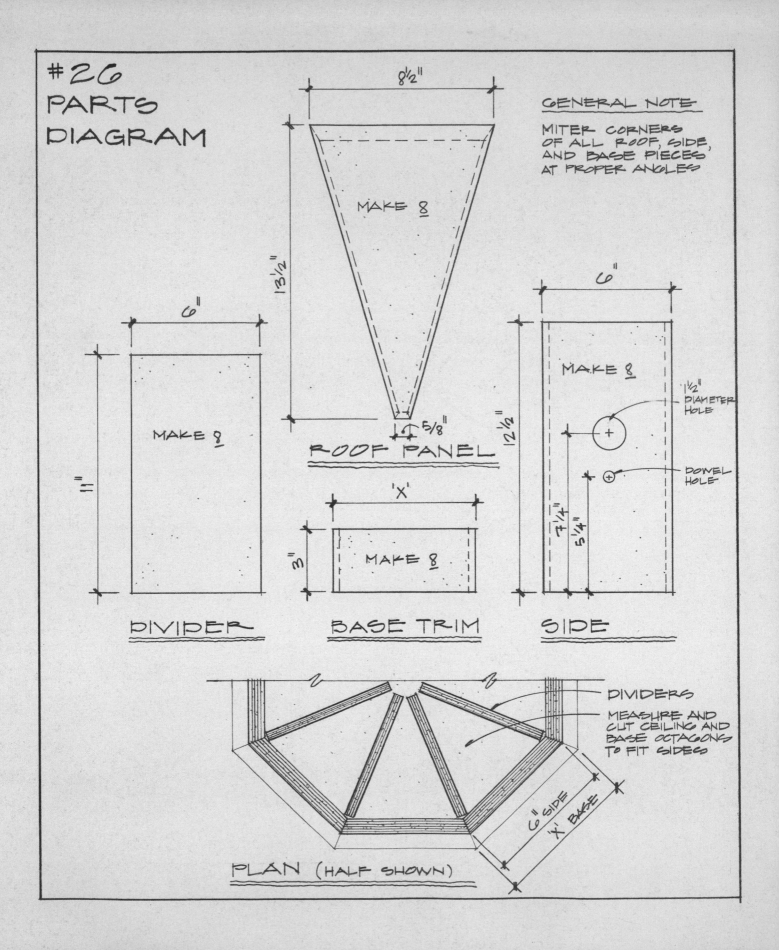

#26
PARTS
DIAGRAM

GENERAL NOTE

MITER CORNERS OF ALL ROOF, SIDE, AND BASE PIECES AT PROPER ANGLES

8½"

MAKE 8

13½"

5/8"

ROOF PANEL

6"

MAKE 8

11"

DIVIDER

'X'

3"

MAKE 8

BASE TRIM

6"

MAKE 8

1½" DIAMETER HOLE

DOWEL HOLE

12½"

7¼"

5¼"

SIDE

DIVIDERS

MEASURE AND CUT CEILING AND BASE OCTAGONS TO FIT SIDES

6" SIDE

'X' BASE

PLAN (HALF SHOWN)

26 TOOLS

Damp rag for glue drips
Drill
Drill bit for entrances and perches
Hammer or screwdriver
Newspaper or plastic sheeting
Saw
Spray bottle and water

SUPPLIES

Clear exterior acrylic or varnish
Latex paint
Nails, screws, or wood staples
OSB
Rough wood boards
Wooden ball
Wooden dowels
Yellow wood glue

INSTRUCTIONS ————————

• Saw the Side pieces with mitered edges from the OSB so that the rough surface is on the outside. Drill the perch and entrance holes. Saw the top and bottom octogonal pieces from OSB. Assemble the interior Dividers to the top and bottom octagons with glue and fasteners.

• The exterior Side pieces can now be attached with glue and fasteners. Try to keep the seams as tight as possible. Fasteners along the top and bottom should be adequate.

• Saw the Base Trim and Roof pieces from the wood boards. Test the Roof pieces as you go to make certain that the angle you are cutting the mitered edge is correct. I find it easier to cut this angle steeper than needed. It will be easier to assemble and, since there is a flat roof below, rain can't get to the chambers. Assemble the Roof and Base Trim pieces using glue and fasteners. You may need to cut a support piece to nail in the center of the Roof to hold it up while you work your way around. You may want to sand the Roof peak flat.

• The decorative wooden ball I used is a curtain rod end that had a screw coming out of the bottom of it. I drilled a pilot hole into the Roof's support piece and screwed the ball in place with glue. Insert the dowels into the perch holes with a dab of glue.

• The paint effect on the Roof and Base Trim pieces of this particular birdhouse was already on the old fence boards from which I built these parts. Once it was all assembled, I painted the whole thing with purple latex paint. I worked the paint well into the texture and grooves with a paintbrush. Before it had a chance to dry, I spritzed it with a water bottle to cause the paint to run. A hose with an adjustable nozzle will work just as well. Obviously this process is best done outside over plastic sheeting or many layers of newspaper.

• If you plan on using this birdhouse outdoors, it is recommended that you coat the entire outside, particularly the walls and entrance hole edges, with clear exterior acrylic or varnish. The OSB will not hold up to weather very well unless protected. This birdhouse can hang from a branch or be mounted on a post.

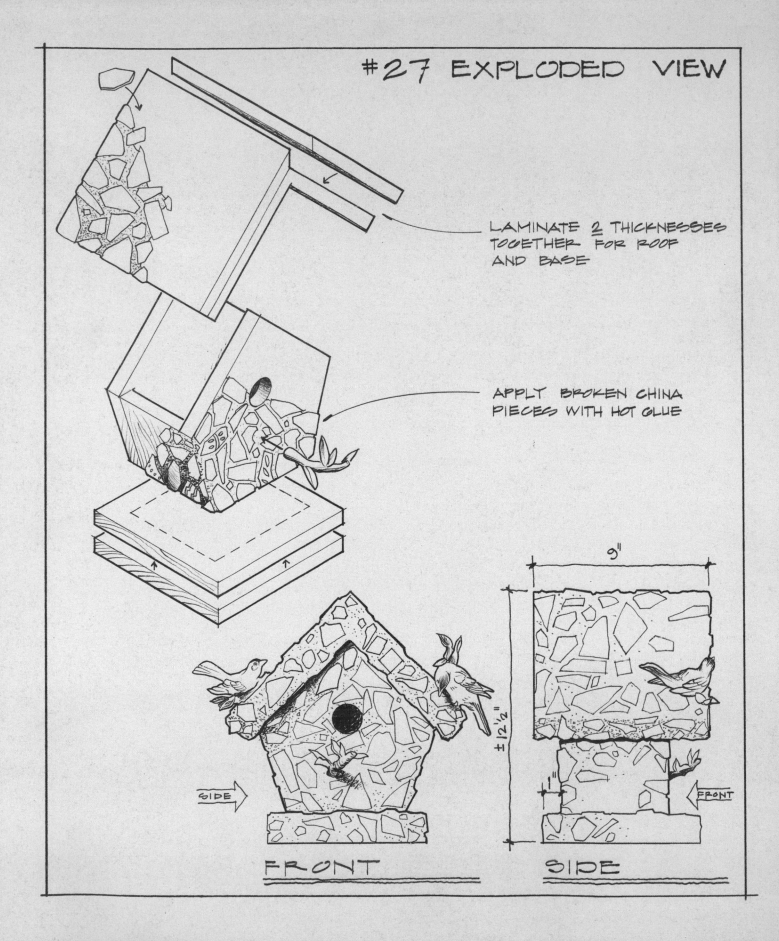

#27 EXPLODED VIEW

LAMINATE 2 THICKNESSES
TOGETHER FOR ROOF
AND BASE

APPLY BROKEN CHINA
PIECES WITH HOT GLUE

9"

± 12½"

1"

½"

SIDE

FRONT

FRONT

SIDE

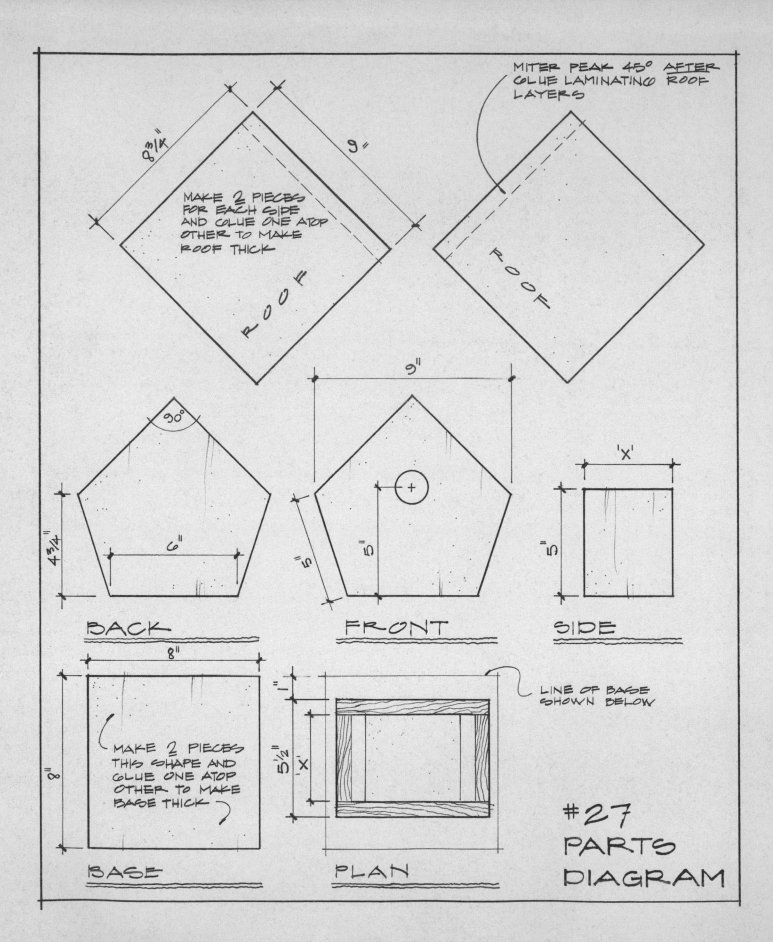

MITER PEAK 45° AFTER GLUE LAMINATING ROOF LAYERS

8 3/4"

9"

MAKE 2 PIECES FOR EACH SIDE AND GLUE ONE ATOP OTHER TO MAKE ROOF THICK

ROOF

ROOF

90°

9"

4 3/4"

6"

5"

5"

5"

'X'

5"

BACK

FRONT

SIDE

8"

8"

MAKE 2 PIECES THIS SHAPE AND GLUE ONE ATOP OTHER TO MAKE BASE THICK

1"

5 1/2"

'X'

LINE OF BASE SHOWN BELOW

BASE

PLAN

#27 PARTS DIAGRAM

27 TOOLS

Drill
Drill bits for entrance and perch
Goggles
Hammer and screwdriver
Hot-glue gun and glue sticks
Saw
Soft cloth or diaper
Work gloves

SUPPLIES

Broken china pieces
Decorative ceramic figurines
Nails, screws, or wood staples
¾" OSB or plywood
Tile grout
Yellow wood glue

INSTRUCTIONS

• Saw all flat parts from the sheet material. Drill the entrance hole in the Front now while the part can be held flat. Assemble the four sides, the Base, and the Roof with fasteners and yellow wood glue. The Roof and Base are each made up of two layers of wood.

• Collect enough china pieces to more than cover all surfaces of the birdhouse. You will be amazed at how much it will take, and you'll want a good assortment to choose from. Ask friends if they will help you collect broken or unusable pieces of china. Garage sales or thrift stores are another great source. Flat pieces, such as plates, work best. Broken bathroom ceramic tiles also work well. Wearing goggles and work gloves, wrap the piece in a cloth and break it into workable pieces by hitting it with the hammer. This part can be fun and stress relieving.

• Antique or secondhand stores are a wonderful source for decorative ceramic figurines. The two ceramic birds perched on the roof of this house previously sat together on an antique vase. Wearing goggles, I used a hammer and screwdriver to gently tap where they joined and break them apart. This can be difficult to predict where to tap, so have a second choice available if you shatter your first. If they break into larger pieces, you can glue them back together. The perch was a branch that was part of the bird figurine.

• Apply a liberal amount of hot glue to the back of each clean, dry piece of china. Take care not to burn or cut yourself. Attach the birds and perch as you work. Try to leave about a ¼" gap between the mosaic pieces. The china must be securely attached or you will have trouble with the next step.

• Apply tile grout, following manufacturer's instructions. It is available in many colors from home improvement stores. Mix it to about the consistency of cake frosting and work it between the china pieces. This part should be done wearing gloves. The edges of broken china are very sharp. Again, be extremely careful not to cut yourself. Keep working with it as it dries by rubbing off any excess with a soft cloth as you go. This part seems to go on forever. Keep rinsing and wringing out your cloth and finish with a clean dry cloth. Buff until the china is clean.

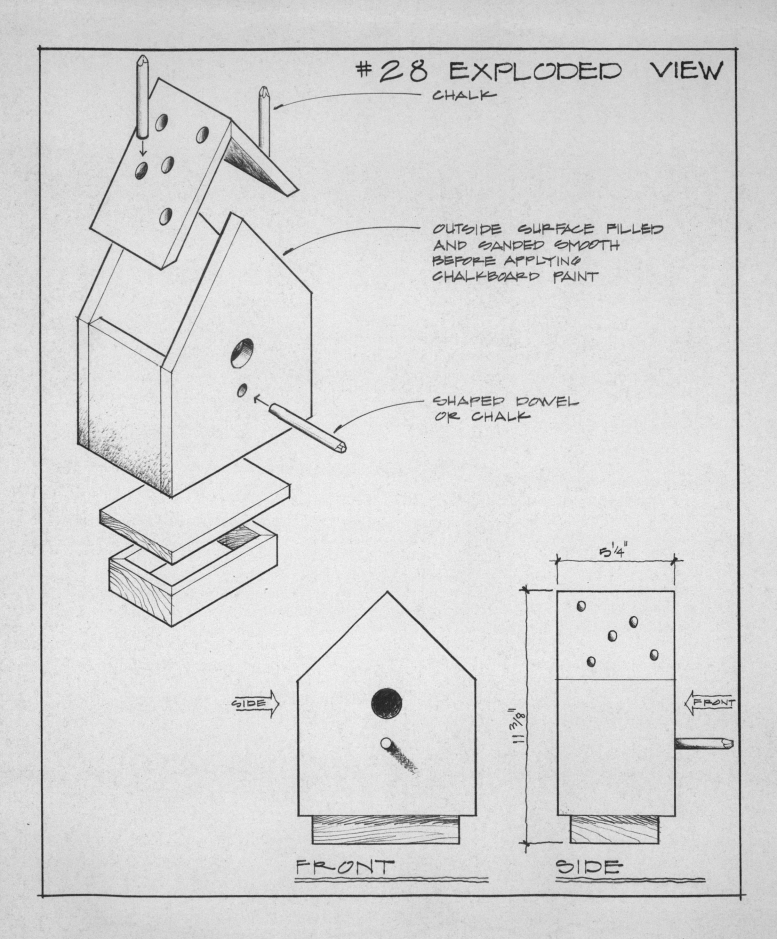

#28 EXPLODED VIEW

CHALK

OUTSIDE SURFACE FILLED
AND SANDED SMOOTH
BEFORE APPLYING
CHALKBOARD PAINT

SHAPED DOWEL
OR CHALK

5¼"

11 3/8"

SIDE

FRONT

FRONT

SIDE

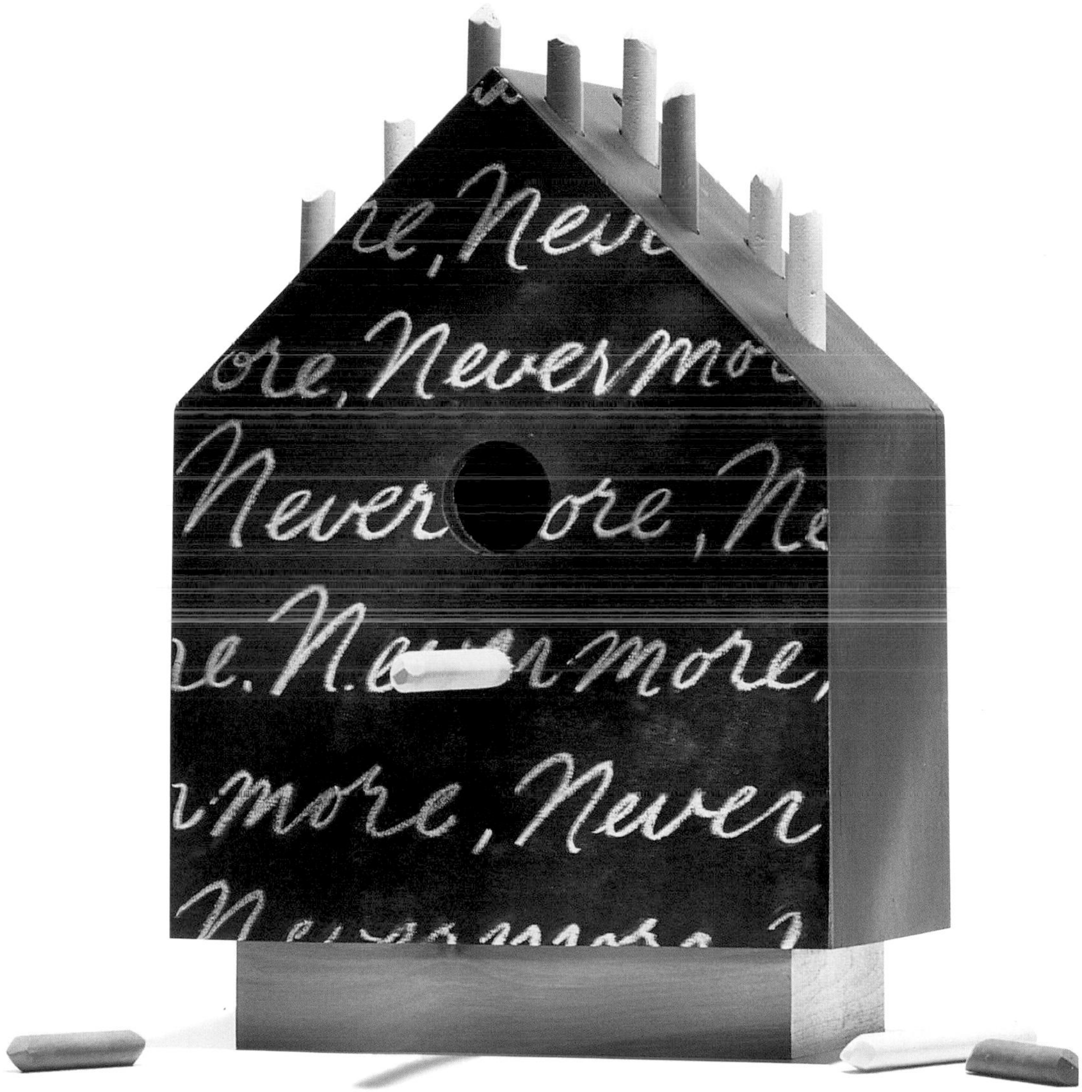
re, Neve
ore, Nevermo
Never ore, Ne
more,
more, Never

#28 PARTS DIAGRAM

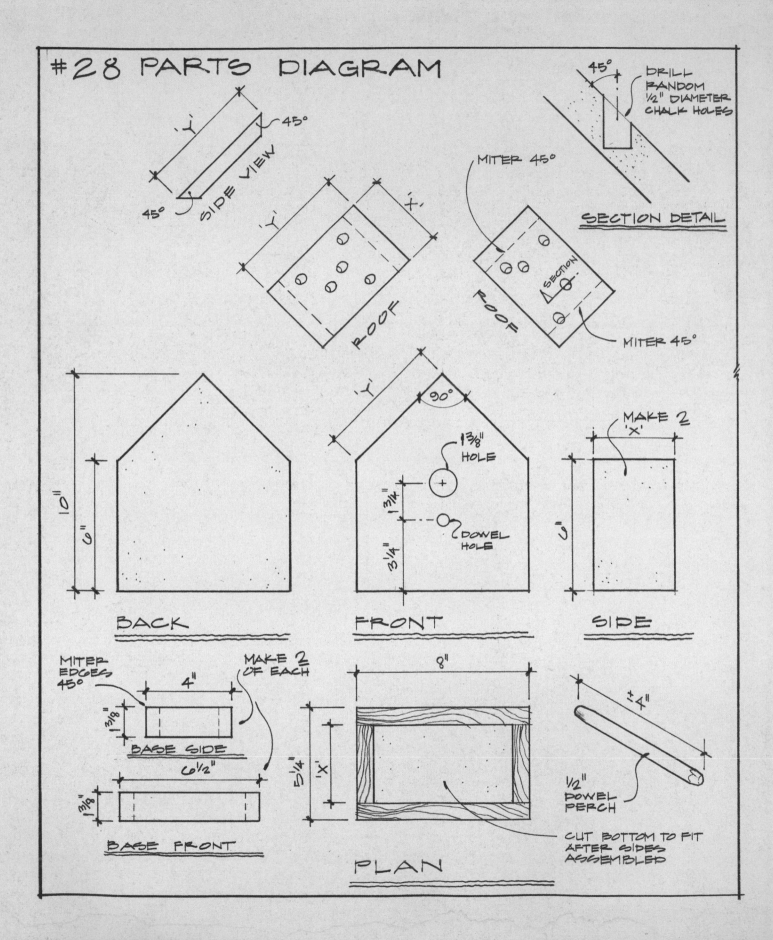

'Y'
45°
SIDE VIEW
45°

45°
DRILL RANDOM ½" DIAMETER CHALK HOLES

SECTION DETAIL

'Y'
'X'
ROOF

MITER 45°
ROOF
SECTION
MITER 45°

10"
6"
BACK

'Y'
90°
1 ⅜" HOLE
3/16"
DOWEL HOLE
3¼"
FRONT

MAKE 2
'X'
6"
SIDE

MITER EDGES 45°
4"
MAKE 2 OF EACH
3/8"
BASE SIDE
6½"
3/8"
BASE FRONT

8"
5¼"
'X'
PLAN

±4"
½" DOWEL PERCH
CUT BOTTOM TO FIT AFTER SIDES ASSEMBLED

28 TOOLS

Damp rag for glue drips
Drill
Drill bit for entrance hole
Hammer or screwdriver
Paintbrush
Router with bit
Sandpaper
Saw

SUPPLIES

Chalk or wooden dowel
Chalkboard paint
Clear acrylic or varnish
MDF or plywood
Nails, screws, or wood staples
Wood base
Wood putty or spackle
Yellow wood glue

INSTRUCTIONS

• Saw the flat pieces from the sheet material. If you use MDF, you will have less trouble cleaning up the edges before you paint, as plywood leaves an exposed grain along the cut edge. Apply glue to each joint as you assemble it. Keep a damp rag handy to wipe up glue drips while they are wet.

• The Base of this birdhouse is a wooden block attached with countersunk screws to the Bottom piece. Wait to attach the Base to the birdhouse until after all the parts have been painted.

• Drill the entrance hole and holes in the Roof to hold the chalk. The Roof holes are best drilled after the birdhouse is assembled. A drill press is really handy here. Drill smaller holes first to avoid creeping with the bit. It can be difficult to drill on a tilted surface, so go slow and easy. Make certain that the chalk you buy will fit in the holes without being too loose. Drill holes in a piece of scrap wood first to check fit. Don't drill the holes all the way through the Roof or the chalk will fall into the birdhouse.

• Fill the nail holes and any gaps and sand the whole birdhouse before painting. The paint technique is relatively simple. Paint the entire birdhouse with chalkboard paint. This type of paint is available at home improvement stores as spray paint or it can be applied with a brush. Apply it evenly, following manufacturer's instructions. It works and looks best if you apply a couple of coats.

• Apply a clear acrylic or varnish to the base. Once the chalkboard paint and varnish are dry you can attach the Base to the birdhouse.

• The perch can be a painted dowel with its end sanded down or a real piece of chalk. If you choose to use a dowel for the perch, insert it with a small dab of glue.

This birdhouse is a great gift for a teacher and also works well for messages by the phone.

127

DEC 1 3 1999

Metric Equivalency Chart

mm-millimetres   cm-centimetres
inches to millimetres and centimetres

inches	mm	cm	inches	cm	inches	cm
⅛	3	0.3	9	22.9	30	76.2
¼	6	0.6	10	25.4	31	78.7
½	13	1.3	12	30.5	33	83.8
⅝	16	1.6	13	33.0	34	86.4
¾	19	1.9	14	35.6	35	88.9
⅞	22	2.2	15	38.1	36	91.4
1	25	2.5	16	40.6	37	94.0
1¼	32	3.2	17	43.2	38	96.5
1½	38	3.8	18	45.7	39	99.1
1¾	44	4.4	19	48.3	40	101.6
2	51	5.1	20	50.8	41	104.1
2½	64	6.4	21	53.3	42	106.7
3	76	7.6	22	55.9	43	109.2
3½	89	8.9	23	58.4	44	111.8
4	102	10.2	24	61.0	45	114.3
4½	114	11.4	25	63.5	46	116.8
5	127	12.7	26	66.0	47	119.4
6	152	15.2	27	68.6	48	121.9
7	178	17.8	28	71.1	49	124.5
8	203	20.3	29	73.7	50	127.0

Index

For the birdhouses, plain text page numbers indicate Exploded Views. *Itallic* page numbers indicate photographs. <u>Underlined</u> page numbers indicate Parts Diagrams. **Boldface** page numbers indicate building instructions.